D0983574

Learning Is Getting Easier

EASE:
Relief from pain or discomfort . . .
to lessen the pressure or tension . . .
to make less difficult . . .
to give freedom

Webster Third New International Dictionary

Learning is Getting Easier

Classrooms Are Becoming More Responsive To Individual Student Needs

S. R. WILSON

D. T. TOSTI, Ph.D.

An Individual Learning Systems Book ILS

Acknowledgements

Chapter 15, *Achieving Flexibility Within Administrative Constraints,* was written by Philip K Jones

Book design by Keith Richardson

Printed in the United States of America

To Fred Keller, who has made it easier for all of us.

Contents

Contents

Introduction

Blasting away at the shortcomings of American education, and particularly of the teachers themselves, has proved a reliable way to sell a lot of books during the last decade. Suggestions ranging from shutting the schools down altogether to carving the graffiti from the school washrooms into the stone over the front entrance, have attracted a great deal of attention and comment. Even the books that purport to offer constructive solutions usually either deal largely with more criticism or suggest approaches that could not possibly be implemented on a large scale within the budgets the taxpayers are willing to finance.

Oddly enough it is fortunate that teachers have left themselves particularly vulnerable to attack. Having been the first to identify the ills of their own institution, they have provided the ammunition for their assailants and left themselves in a poor position to maintain that the ills don't exist. We call this "fortunate" because, having faced their own problems first, they were also the leaders in the efforts to do something about them. While others criticized, the teachers themselves sought practicable solutions that could be implemented within the constraints imposed by taxpayers, legislative policies, and critics.

This book is the result of a deliberate and systematic effort to find out how the teachers have solved their own problems in their own classrooms. It is focused principally on *the changes teachers are making that permit them to adapt the instructional system ever more frequently and accurately to satisfy the personal needs of each individual student*. This, we understand, is very nearly universally accepted as a desirable trend in education and we wanted to find out how teachers were approaching that particular goal. We were impressed with what we saw.

In this book, we are not trying for dramatic effect. There are no images of blinking lights, buzzing tape decks, or clicking computer terminals. Those are innovations that schools cannot afford on the massive scale needed, even when they can be proved to increase learning effectiveness. Rather, the image is of a teacher in a classroom or office trying to modify the system to increase his or her ability to fulfill the personal needs of each student. In short, this book describes what happens between teachers and students. It treats, one by one, the main problems teachers face in trying to serve individual students better and describes the solutions they have found.

Anyone who wishes to predict future trends in education would be well advised to look at the innovative systems now in use in classrooms rather than attending to the sensational (and often conflicting) forecasts of those who propose to tear the present system apart. Teachers everywhere are more likely to trust, and adopt, innovations that have been tested and found effective by their colleagues in classroom experience than those that have been proved in experiments under controlled conditions—or worse, only proposed in theoretical constructs. In a very real sense, this book represents our forecast of the wave of the future for education, which we found by looking on the campuses of today.

RESPONSIVENESS DEFINED

Throughout the research, organization, and preparation of the content of this book, we have stuck single-mindedly to one basic objective. We started with the assumption that there is one common element in all the conflicting statements as to what is desirable in education, and our entire focus has been on learning the extent to which that universally desired condition is already realized in the nation's educational system. In generally recognizable terms this condition can be described as follows:

The educational system should be as responsive as possible to the needs of each individual student.

There is an enormous amount of disagreement as to *what students need* and the point at which the educational system has become responsive *enough* to those needs. These are perfectly legitimate arguments, but the trouble is that there is no such thing as an authoritative statement.

On the first question (what the students' needs are) the argument usually hinges around opinions as to what human beings require for happiness, fulfillment, citizenship, and so on. In this area, no one is any more of an authority than anyone else, so the arguments go on endlessly without very much happening one way or another.

As to the second question (how much responsiveness is "enough") there is again no authoritative position. For the purposes of this book, therefore, we simply recognize the universal opinion that there should be more than there is. We have never heard or read of a teacher, critic, parent, political leader, or student who would not agree with that fundamental assertion.

As stated, however, the assertion that there should be more responsiveness than there is does not provide a basis for a very systematic assessment of the current condition. The term responsiveness needs to be defined in more precise terms if it is to be recognized when it appears. Is the educational system responsive, for example, in a free school environment where all students are allowed to do exactly as they please? Our reply to this question would be that such a condition does not describe an educational system at all, no matter how responsive, and would therefore fall outside the scope of this book. We are talking about the *educational system* and not about a student's total learning environment. We are concerned with what goes on within the formal structure that has been established to provide students with the skills society thinks they need.

As a basis for our research, we have established one criterion which, as far as we know, everyone would agree can be used to evaluate the responsiveness of an educational system. *We assume here that the system is responsive whenever some part of the instructional sequence can be modified to accommodate the recognized special needs of an individual student.* Any condition in which all students must do the same thing with the same materials at the same time is not responsive. Every time, however, that a technique or approach is introduced which increases the frequency with which the instructional sequence can be changed for one student, that technique or approach represents a step in the direction of responsiveness. Our purpose in this book is to report on the types of such steps that have been developed and proved to be practicable in actual classroom experience. What we want to know is how frequently and accurately the instructional sequence *can* be changed. What changes *will* be made, and how often, depend on the needs of the students themselves, and those needs are infinitely variable.

HOW TO USE THIS BOOK

This book is intended to serve two types of readers. One is the reader (a teacher) who has grappled with some or all of these problems in the classroom and who wants to see what other teachers have done in particular areas. For this type of reader, we have tried to make each chapter complete in itself so that the techniques described can be understood without reference to materials contained elsewhere in the book. In this sense, the book can be used as a reference document in which teachers can use the table of contents to find alternative solutions to individual problems with which they may be faced.

The second category of readers encompasses all those (teachers, parents, or anyone else interested in education) who want a total perspective on the progress that has been made toward the overall goal of responsiveness in the educational system. These may be teachers who have had only casual exposure to the techniques that have been touted under the heading of individualized instruction, or interested parents who would like to exercise a more constructive influence at meetings of the school board. These readers will find it useful to start at the beginning and work straight through the book. For the reader who is not already familiar with the problems of individualized instruction it will be preferable to follow the sequence of topics in the order in which they are presented. It will help, for example, to be acquainted with the nature and function of learning objectives before reviewing the types of instructional management that are used in developing classroom procedures.

Thus the book is intended not only as a reference document for those who already have experience with individualization, but also as an overview of the total process of making the system responsive to individual student needs. We would like to acknowledge at the start that we have not presented every technique and classroom management procedure that has been devised and tested. There are far too many of them to be covered in one book, so we have limited ourselves to those that have achieved the most widespread use. We would also like to stipulate that not all techniques and approaches are equally useful in all situations. In each case we have presented alternative solutions in the hope that the teacher will be able to find one that fits his or her particular situation. The authors, however, do have preferences which are stated in the form of recommendations at the end of each chapter.

CONCLUSION

We are not trying to defend the educational system; we do not suggest that criticisms of education are "unfair." The teachers themselves don't usually suggest that criticism is unwarranted. We only remind the reader that this book describes what teachers are doing. Admittedly these practices are not yet universal; there is much left to be done. After finishing the book, however, one might find it interesting to look for comparable reforms anywhere, in industrial management or in the archaic practices of government.

We submit that the progress already made within the educational system toward the universally accepted goal of responsiveness compares favorably with achievements in other social institutions.

Of one thing we are absolutely convinced. In another decade or so, when we look back to see what revolution actually took place in education, it will look very much like what is happening in thousands of classrooms already.

1

Taking Some Of The Guesswork Out Of Motivation

Of all the possible ways in which a student might be influenced by greater responsiveness in education, the effect on his motivation is by far the most frequently mentioned. Improved student motivation (or better, the elimination of conditions that tend to destroy his natural motivation) is the most popular single reason cited for the need to be more responsive to individual student needs. We know of no one, including the students themselves, who would contend that any student ever works up to the full limit of his capability. Thus, in any book about responsiveness (indeed, in any book about any aspect of education) the subject of motivation must receive considerable attention.

This book is no exception. There is not the slightest question in our minds that of the technical and procedural changes taking place in the nation's classrooms, increased motivation has had the greatest single impact on students. Each change that has been made to make teaching more responsive to student needs has, in fact, increased the intensity and frequency with which students do the things that make them successful learners.

Thus, throughout the book, we will be highlighting over and over the relationship between specific changes in classroom procedures and the resulting effect on the behavior of the students. Our approach in these discussions, however, differs substantially from the treatment that the subject of motivation receives in most books on education. At no point in the book will we discuss the *intrinsic* motivations of the students themselves; nor will we ascribe any intrinsic motivating properties to any particular learning activity.

This does not mean that we deny either the existence or the importance of the intrinsic motivations a student brings with him into the classroom. They do exist and they are of paramount importance to a teacher or an instructional systems designer who has to decide what material, activities and events should be built into the school and classroom environment. One of the greatest drawbacks of the concept of equal education is that it tends to be taken to mean that the same environments, the same activities, the same learning materials, the same teacher skills and the same learning objectives must be maintained for all students, regardless of the differences in their intrinsic motivation. Perhaps the most important reason for treating students differently is to provide systematically for recognition of these differences.

Our reason for not talking about the intrinsic motivations of students isn't that we don't think they are important but that we know of no way to describe them in meaningful terms (neither, as far as we know, does anyone else). We can, however, describe meaningfully the observable behavior of students from which people draw their conclusions about the underlying motivation. For example, a student who frowns a great deal, starts fights frequently, stares out the window, is often absent from class, and who fails to complete his work on time is likely to earn the reputation of being poorly motivated. On the other hand, a student who smiles a lot, participates in group activities, spends most of his time looking at the teacher, is punctual in meeting required schedules, and completes his tasks rapidly is very likely to be considered a highly motivated student. While we would never deny that these behaviors are influenced by intrinsic qualities of the student, we have to admit honestly that we don't know how to describe those intrinsic qualities. We do know, however, that any shift from the first pattern of behavior to the second is likely to make the student a more successful learner and to be popularly seen as evidence of a higher level of motivation.

Therefore, we will report frequently in the following chapters on the changes in student behaviors that are seen to *follow* changes in the instructional management procedures employed in the classroom. It is quite clear that many teachers are using much less guesswork in increasing the frequency of successful behaviors (which one interprets as better motivation) than used to be the case when it was felt that behavior could only be changed by influencing directly the inner motivation itself. Our report here will be concerned with the observed changes in student behavior; we leave it to the reader to draw any conclusions he likes about the interpretation of those changes in terms of changed motivation.

WHO MODIFIES BEHAVIOR?

Those individuals who are concerned with the motivation of behavior go by many names, such as: therapist, teacher, parent, counselor. We find the term *manager* to be most appropriate for those who deal with the contingencies affecting behavior.

We are all behavior managers. In an intrinsic sense it is an inescapable requirement that we manage our own behavior. In an extrinsic sense it is inescapable since we are a part of the verbal community that shapes the behavior of all members of that community. We are managers of our own behavior when we attempt to reform our habits, to keep schedules, to meet personal objectives, to develop skills that will enhance our ability to interact with our environment, and to sharpen our ability to discriminate that which is relevant to our own personal brand of wisdom. We are managers of the behavior of others when we attempt to convince them to believe as we do, when we teach them useful skills, and when we interact with those who are dependent upon us until they can manage for themselves. The responsibility is enormous — and if any problem exists in regard to this responsibility it is in the fact that there are too few people who can manage their own behavior (much less that of others) rather than in the supposition that no systematic method for the management of behavior has been found. It has. It is easy to learn and, with a little practice, relatively easy to apply.

COMMON CHARACTERISTICS OF THE MOST EFFECTIVE CLASSROOM BEHAVIOR MANAGEMENT

The changes that are desired in student behavior and the techniques that are employed in bringing those changes about are as many and varied as the people involved. The specific changes one wants to see in a student depend on what he is doing now and what is wanted. How one brings about any particular change depends on what it is that turns that particular student on, as well as the personality and perspective of the person who is trying to help. But those efforts that turn out to be successful in bringing about a desired change have certain characteristics in common.

By knowing what these common characteristics are, one can examine any particular change (past or proposed) in a student's environment and predict the probable effect on a student's behavior. To take a simple and obvious example, if a student is ridiculed by his peers as an "apple polisher" when he volunteers for additional classroom tasks, this extra effort is likely to decline; the consequences of that behavior do not increase the probability that it will occur again. On the other hand, if a fellow student makes admiring comments about the quality of his work, he is more likely to extend himself to produce high-quality work in the future.

Basically, then, the points of similarity between the most successful behavior management approaches lie in the way the behavior manager arranges the consequences of the behavior that is observed in the classroom. Within that general statement, however, there are several more detailed similarities that can be seen.

Consequences Are Controlled Systematically

The concept that a relationship exists between behavior and its consequences is not a new idea. The fact that lights go on or off when a switch is flipped maintains the behavior of switch-flipping. The fact that we receive a paycheck as a consequence of spending a given number of hours a day at work increases the probability that those hours will be spent in that pursuit. Everyone who has rewarded some behavior and punished others knows that what happens after the behavior occurs increases or decreases the probability that it will be repeated. Yet, basically, it is merely by taking this rule seriously enough to apply it *systematically* that it is possible to increase our effectiveness as behavior managers.

The trouble with the relationship between behavior and its consequences is that it is a natural law, and the problem with natural laws is that they work all the time, making no distinction as to whether they are operated systematically or haphazardly. The most successful behavior management is carried out by those who are always conscious that this natural law is at work and who try always to arrange the relationships in a way that produces the most desirable behaviors in themselves and others.

When a random relationship between behaviors and consequences is allowed to occur, without any systematic planning, there are certain to be many instances in which the consequences will tend to strengthen (or reinforce) *undesired* behavior. We make no value judgments here as to what is "good" or "bad" behavior; we only make the observation that a haphazard arrangement of consequences often reinforces behavior we don't like. We think it is logical, then, to suggest that careful and systematic attention to the arrangement of the relationship between behaviors and their consequences is more likely to produce behaviors that are desired; and, the logic of this hypothesis is verified by the fact that the most successful classroom behavior managers are those who pay the greatest attention to the relationship.

Consequences Are Ranked According To Their Relative Desirability For Each Student

We stated earlier that we would not ascribe any intrinsically motivating properties to any activity or event. We know that some activities have more widespread popularity than others but we know of no activity that is inherently motivating for everyone. A trip to the zoo has more widespread appeal as a motivator than a poke in the eye with a sharp stick, but that does not mean that everyone will work harder to earn a trip to the zoo, no matter how intrinsically motivating that activity may appear to the teacher.

Certainly, in deciding what consequences will be made available in order to reinforce the probability of desired behavior, one should select first those that have the most widespread appeal. What happens too often, however, is that the popularity of each alternative is considered from the point of view of the teacher (i.e., the behavior manager) rather than the student. The question isn't what reinforces the teacher but, rather, what reinforces the student.

One of the best ways to assess several alternative consequences, in terms of their relative reinforcing qualities for any particular student or any group of students, is to find out what the students are most likely to do if they are given the freedom to choose. Those that come at the top of this list are called high probability behaviors and those at the bottom are called low probability behaviors.

It must always be remembered, however, that these have to be identified as the behaviors that are high or low probability *for the students* and not for the teachers. As will be seen later in this book, it frequently happens that the scheduling of consequences changes considerably when they are viewed from this perspective.

The Desired Behaviors Are Described In Precise Terms

The most successful classroom managers are always careful to make very precise decisions as to the behavior they want. The behaviors may be expressed in such terms as: achieving specific learning objectives, punctuality in instructor conferences, type and frequency of responses in group discussions, or completion of extra enrichment activities. Each instructor makes evaluations of student performance against his or her own set of criteria as to what behaviors are the most important. Naturally there are some behaviors that almost all teachers would desire; but there are individual differences in the ranking of priorities, depending both on the teacher who is making the evaluation, and the normal pattern of behavior exhibited by the student.

The most successful behavior managers (i.e., those who are most often able to elicit the behavior they desire from their students) are those who know precisely what they want. Those who have the least effect on the behavior of their students are typically those who express their desires only in such terms as developing an interest in the subject matter, or demonstrating a desire to learn. Precise specification of the desired behavior also helps the student, who is more likely to earn the consequences *he* desires if he knows what is expected of him. This is one of the biggest reasons for setting precise learning objectives (which is discussed more fully in Chapter 3).

The Most Desirable Consequences Are Made Contingent On Demonstration Of The Desired Behavior

This is simply one of the many ways in which each of us restates "Grandma's Law" in all our daily interactions. The phrase, "After you eat your beans you may have ice cream," can be restated as:

- Clean up your room and then you may go outside and play.
- If you work ten hours a day instead of eight you will receive a bonus.
- After you have shown me you can spell "tricycle," you may ride it.
- If you complete the requirements of this course early, you will be excused from class attendance for the remainder of the term.
- After you have completed a specified amount of low probability behavior, you will be permitted an appropriate amount of high probability behavior.

All of these statements of Grandma's Law (with the possible exception of the last generalized expression of it) are familiar to everyone. All the Law says is that we can get students, or anyone else, to perform tasks that may not interest them very much if the performance of those tasks is followed by an opportunity to do something they enjoy more.

Grandma would probably be astonished to see how frequently this seemingly obvious sequence of events is taken in exactly the reverse order. We seem constantly to be giving the command, "After you finish the high probability behavior you must then complete a large chunk of low probability behavior." For example, we have all heard the injunction, "One more television program, then you have to do your homework." The same inversion is at work when we ignore a student until he does something bizarre.

RECOMMENDATIONS

As we stated earlier, we will be dealing throughout the remainder of this book with changes in techniques and instructional management procedures that have proved most effective in getting students to do the things that make them successful learners. This is the way we recognize that a change in motivation has occurred. The effectiveness of any of these practices — or any others — can be evaluated in terms of the four criteria that have been described in this chapter:

- Systematic control of consequences
- Ranking the desirability of alternative consequences from a student's perspective
- Deciding precisely what behavior is desired
- Making the most desirable consequences contingent on the desired behavior

There is nothing difficult or obscure about these criteria and success in behavior management is not a result of inspiration or genius. Those who make the most systematic use of the natural laws of behavior (which are known to everyone) are the ones who are most frequently able to help their students become successful learners.

The most effective behavior managers regularly ask themselves three questions:

1. What happens to a student when he does something I like?

2. What happens to him when he does something I don't like?

3. How can I rearrange the consequences to increase the number of times the things he likes happen *after* the things I like?

2

The Accountability Concept In Education

The very nearly universal demand for greater responsiveness to individual student needs is invariably justified on the basis of a general statement that responsiveness is ''good'' for students. After all, what could be more logical than to conclude that students are better served by a system which is tailored more directly to their individual needs? Thus, for practical purposes, responsiveness in education is usually considered an end in itself.

This intuitive judgment may be adequate to establish a generally accepted direction for changes in education, but it isn't of much value to an instructor who must make a specific decision to adopt or not to adopt a given change in materials or classroom procedures. To a conscientious instructor, responsiveness — or to use the more popular buzz word, ''individualization'' — cannot be considered an end in itself. The instructor must be convinced that the particular change under consideration will contribute something to the student that is not available in current classroom procedures *and at a cost the system can afford.*

The teacher who tries to undertake such an analysis, however, has a difficult problem. Trying to find out what additional benefit the student might derive from a changed procedure is difficult when there is no meaningful way to describe the benefit the students are deriving prior to the change. We tend to define the output of the educational process in terms of the characteristics of a graduate, e.g., an educated citizen, a thinking or rational man, a high achiever or a valuable contributor to society. In other words, we define the output from education in terms of a totality of qualities, any one of which may or may not have been influenced significantly by the fact that the individual spends a given number of years in contact with the educational process.

Gradually, however, this focus is beginning to change. There is increasing emphasis on the concept that an educational institution exists for the purpose of creating in its students the maximum gain between point of entry and point of departure. This concept has been termed Educational Accountability. Accountability assumes that the evaluation of any educational process, whether it is one in use or a new one under consideration, requires more than a description of the skills of its graduates. For example, schools that set high performance standards for graduation are usually the same schools that set high performance standards for admission. It is a hotly debated point as to whether the high standards are achieved through excellence in teaching or by a process of screening out in advance all but the most capable students. The point will go on being debated, without resolution, until it is possible to isolate, and describe, the effect of the educational process on the student.

In any event, before an instructor can assess objectively any proposed changes in media or classroom procedures, it is necessary to assess the gain achieved by students with the proposed system compared with the one currently in use. The question is: "How much 'value' is added to the student under each of the alternative procedures?"

This is a good deal more than an academic question for students, instructors, and taxpayers. Each of these three groups is putting a sizable investment into the educational process and they are all becoming increasingly interested in knowing what that investment produces. More particularly they want to know what they are receiving compared with what they would get from a different investment, or no investment at all.

The investment by the students represents, on average, about 1,000 hours per year for 12 to 16 years and the sacrifice of whatever benefit they might derive from using that time in other activities. The fact that some students leave the system with a high level of qualifications is clearly attributable to a combination of factors, including the education to which they have been exposed, home environment, cultural environment, and so on. It may be that they derive a significant portion of the total ''value added'' from the schools but that would be difficult to prove. On the other hand, there are students who put in the same investment of time but whose achievement demonstrates that the schools they attend serve principally a custodial function. There are enough cases in which youngsters receive a high school diploma with a fourth or fifth grade reading level to demonstrate the point. From the standpoint of a student who gets very little from his investment in schooling, therefore, the question of value added from education has very practical significance.

From the teacher's standpoint the ''product''of education (the value added to the student) also has some practical implications. Certainly the teacher's investment in training is greater than that required for most careers but, at least until recently, increases in teachers' salaries have not kept pace with the national averages of personal incomes. In a society which tries (not always successfully) to relate compensation to productivity, an inability to define their output places the teachers at something of a disadvantage. The investments they make in their careers are not generally as highly rewarded financially as an investment in other industries, so they must find satisfaction in observing their impact on their students; again an application of the *value added* concept. This issue is becoming even more serious now with enrollments dropping, a diminishing supply of teaching positions, increasing financial pressure on the schools, and the newly developing emphasis on teaching accountability.

Finally there are the implications for those who pay the bills. Any type of change instituted across the board in a system as vast as education has a very large financial impact on the country as a whole. Annual expenditures on formal education in the United States are now exceeding $75 billion to serve 60 million students (each of whom spends roughly 1,000 hours per year in the educational system). On a worldwide basis, these figures (give or take 25%) are in the neighborhood of $300 billion for 500 million students. Even a small percentage change, either in the value added to the product or in the cost of producing the product in an industry of this size, has vast implications. In almost every country in the world, except for the U.S., the cost of education is the largest single component of the gross national product.

For all these reasons, the concept of accountability in education is the subject of continually increasing attention. In fact, it is becoming a whole area of expertise in itself. Generally it is reflected in two types of approaches that are receiving fairly widespread publicity:

1. The most popular approach, as exemplified in performance contracting, is now receiving occasional mention in popular magazines and newspapers. By this approach, students are tested to establish their grade level of achievement in each subject matter area at the beginning, and again at the end, of some time period. The people who are responsible for maintaining the system are then paid according to the grade gain recorded between the two examinations. This type of data is better than nothing, but it is still only a very rough measure of the relative effectiveness of two systems. There are too many variables that change simultaneously in these types of comparisons.

2. A less popular, but more precise, measure of the instructional effectiveness of alternative materials, media, or classroom procedures is a device known as the "G Statistic" (G standing for gain). By this device, a student's achievement during a particular course is expressed as a *percent* of the total gain he could have made during the course. The procedure for determining the statistic is as follows:

- On entering the course, the student is given an examination equal to the final examination in content and difficulty. For example, a student might take the examination and demonstrate 20% mastery before starting the course. This would mean that his possible gain, if he scores 100% on the final after taking the course, is 80%.

- The student takes the final examination again after completing the course to see what level of mastery he has achieved. To continue with the same example, if a student scores 90% on the final exam, his actual gain as a result of taking the course would be 70% (the 90% on the final minus the 20% he had already achieved before entering the course).
- The G Statistic, which is his actual gain as a percent of the total possible gain, is 88% (or 70% divided by 80%). This device is not as useful for large "chunks" of progress as the procedure described in number one above but it gives a more precise measure of the comparative "value added" between alternative procedures and materials. The measure has enough credibility that its results are difficult to ignore. When a teacher can show that his students were in the 98th percentile in terms of gain achieved, others pay a good deal of attention.

The effort to focus on accountability in education has so far been limited to relatively small increments of value added by way of student progress in cognitive learning. Instructors and others interested in education would like to have meaningful measures of the effect of education over longer periods of time and in wider ranges of subject matter, and they would like to find techniques which would provide meaningful descriptions of the influence of progress in areas other than cognitive learning. What has been done so far is only a start, and the sophistication of the measurement techniques will undoubtedly improve. It will become possible to measure the effect of more variables over longer periods of time.

To us, however, the important point is that the accountability concept is now established in two significant types of applications and its use is growing rapidly. The knowledge gained regarding the effect on students of alternative instructional approaches and of the educational system in total is likely to have a significant effect on the specific types of changes in education in the future. *The systems, media, materials, and skills that can be shown to have the greatest learning effectiveness at the lowest cost will achieve the most widespread adoption.*

3

Selecting Learning Objectives

One basic requirement for any useful response to a student's needs must be an ability to evaluate what the student has actually done *recently*. Much of the content of this book is concerned with the procedures and techniques teachers have used in carrying out the observations of student performance from which evaluations are to be made. But, there are two components of evaluation; the observed performance itself *and* the performance that was expected. It is difficult to decide what a student needs on the basis of observation alone. This difficulty has led instructors to take a first step — development of clear learning objectives in terms of behaviors expected of the students — before worrying about observation and evaluation.

"Behavioral Objectives Are No Damn Good" is the title of a paper by James Evans (1969). Evans' point is that if one already has a valid way of evaluating student accomplishment, either through objective or subjective means, then the generation of precise learning objectives to specify the required student behavior is a superfluous exercise. The fly in Evans' ointment is that most instructors do not feel that the performance standards they presently use are effective. Also, the growing concern for accountability is bringing increased pressure for teachers to specify, before they begin to teach, just what they intend to accomplish. Therefore, the development of objectives is often a desirable, or even necessary, activity.

The primary purpose of an instructional objective is to specify exactly what the student is to learn in a way that will permit verification that it has been taught. This is no small accomplishment. Few instructors so far have attempted to reconcile the expectations of their educational goals with the realities of their final exams.

There are other ancillary benefits that may be derived from preparing objectives. Those most often cited are:

1. They provide an aid in selecting or designing instructional materials.

2. They may be used as a guide for students in independent study programs.

3. They lay out the "rules of the game" for students by indicating what they will be held accountable for.

These benefits may be important in some programs, but a behavioral objective is primarily a generalized evaluation item, and hence must be justified in terms of its primary purpose, i.e., assessing student performance. In its simplest form, a behavioral objective specifies what information the students will be given, and the appropriate types of responses.

Most objectives indicate some sort of *observable* behavior. This requirement is made in order to reduce ambiguity. Deciding exactly how specific a series of objectives should be is often a problem. One may easily go to extremes in either direction, from too specific (such as observation of minute muscle movements) to the very general (employing terms like *appreciate* or *understand*). The most useful guideline can be stated as follows:

> The objective should be stated in only enough detail to enable several knowledgeable observers to agree that the observed student behavior represents an adequate accomplishment of that objective.

CHARACTERISTICS OF OBJECTIVES

Objectives vary along two dimensions: form and complexity. The major forms are:

1. *Cognitive*: Those dealing with acquisition of knowledge or verbal skills and reasoning.

2. *Affective*: Those dealing with emotional and attitudinal behaviors.

3. *Motor*: Those dealing with skills involving the muscles, such as bicycle riding.

In this chapter we deal primarily with cognitive objectives since these are the types of behaviors most commonly pursued in academic settings.

The other dimension is that of complexity. Many taxonomies present schemes for developing hierarchies of complexity. Such systems rank objectives from *simple* (such as those involved in ''fact'' learning) to *complex* (such as those involved in analyzing implications of a concept in a multitude of settings). Most theorists assume that complex behaviors are built from lower-level skills. This assumption makes it necessary, in pursuing complex objectives, to develop lower order (simpler) objectives first.

This approach sometimes leads to problems. If lower order objectives are developed first, they may tend to limit the scope of the course. However, teachers usually find that the overwhelming majority of academically-oriented objectives for which they test in existing classrooms are, in fact, found at the lower levels of complexity. In most cases, therefore, developing simpler objectives first is a practicable approach.

In this chapter we describe the four basic types of objectives encountered at the lower order range of complexity:

1. Recall (definition)
2. Discrimination (comparison)
3. Generalization (problem identification)
4. Problem solving

Recall

In recall, a specific stimulus requires a specific response from the student. Students may be asked to complete rules, give definitions, or otherwise recall specific information. Sample criterion items are:

Who was the first president of the United States?

What are the definite attributes of a triangle?

In a recall objective, the students are usually given a definition of, description of, purpose for, or use of some concept *X*, and their response may be to identify that concept at the instructor's request. Or the objective may be stated in the reverse order, i.e., given concept *X*, the student will define it.

The following is a general form which may be used in constructing recall objectives. (A multiple-choice format is used here but any response format may be employed.)

GENERAL FORM: Given the instruction to define concept X, the student will select from several choices a definition of X similar to the following: "X..."

(NOTE: The third part, "similar to the following," is optional.)

EXAMPLE: When given the instruction to define the term "acquisition," the student will select from several choices the correct definition.

Discrimination

Discrimination implies comparison. This is an extremely important class of objectives and one which is often neglected. The first step in any analytical procedure involves discrimination. For example, a small child must first learn to pay attention to the number of sides of a figure before he can grasp the concept of triangularity. At a more advanced level, the same principle is used when a student is given a series of geometric figures and asked to infer their common or differentiating properties. He may be given a series of regular polygons and asked how they are alike. The compare-and-contrast kind of essay question is another way of evaluating a discrimination objective.

In a discrimination task, the student may be given the instruction to evaluate the relationship among, determine the definite attributes of, or contrast and compare several classes of ideas or things:

GENERAL FORM: When asked to evaluate the relationship among X, Y, . . . N, the student will select from several choices the paragraph which best describes this relationship.

EXAMPLE: When asked to identify the difference between retroactive and proactive inhibition, the student will select, from several choices, the paragraph which describes this difference.

Generalization

In generalization, the student is assumed to have learned a concept when he can select examples of that concept from an array of alternatives. For example, when shown a picture of several geometric figures, the student should be able to identify those which are triangles.

There are many forms for generalization. The student may be given a rule or principle and then asked to give examples of that principle. The objective may be stated in an inductive form, so that the student would be given a series of examples and told to infer the rule.

The general form is as follows:

GENERAL FORM: Given examples of an X, the student will be able to select from several choices the example which illustrates principle Y

EXAMPLE: When given several versions of the same communication, the student will select the version which contains the least amount of redundancy.

Problem Solving

Given a problem situation, the student should either select from a series of alternatives the appropriate solution or construct an appropriate solution, while considering guiding principles or algorithms.

The general form of this objective specifies the class of problems and their solutions and indicates the principle, rule or algorithm by which the student would solve the problem. It is important to state the principle in the objective, even though it does not appear in the actual evaluation item.

GENERAL FORM: Given a problem situation which is an example of class X, the student will select from several choices the correct approach to the situation, using principle Y.

(NOTE: The third part, using principle Y, may be omitted if the objective is unambiguous.)

EXAMPLE: When asked to evaluate a situation in which there is an apparent failure in communication, the student will select from several choices the description which indicates the appropriate action of a leader who assumes responsibility for the failure in communication.

RECOMMENDATION

The most economical use of time and effort in this area is achieved by starting with what is already known, i.e., the test items for the course. The first step is to translate these into specific learning objectives, grouping them according to the four forms indicated in this chapter. Later, one may prepare more complex objectives, if they are needed, which build upon those previously generated.

Behavioral learning objectives are useful in demonstrating what the course actually attempts to teach, and giving a basis for evaluating its teaching effectiveness.

But one should avoid overdoing it; objectives should be prepared, but not deified. When the instructor is satisfied that the objectives are an accurate reflection of what he wants to teach, further effort can be spent to better advantage in developing good test items.

Finally, it is worth noting that there are a number of objective "banks" covering subject matter ranging from calculus to the social development of two year olds, to cosmetology. When behavioral objectives are needed a great deal of effort may be saved by examining the contents of these banks.

4

Types Of Instructional Management

In response to our survey, teachers gave a variety of reasons for moving toward individualization, ranging from "student self reliance" to "desperation." But, for whatever reasons, more and more teachers are committing themselves to some degree of individualization in their classrooms. Professional magazines are full of articles on individualization, extolling its merits and defining its attributes, usually in terms of expensive media, independent study, or special tutoring which few schools can afford. In fact, the absence of any of these attributes does not mean that an educational experience is not individualized.

It is useless to try to make an exact distinction between those instructional programs that are individualized, and those that are not. The most one can say is that one program is *more*, or *less*, individualized than another. Individualized instruction occurs to a greater or lesser extent in every classroom. Whenever an instructor stops to modify his presentation because of a student's query, that student (but not necessarily the others in the room) is receiving a form of individualized instruction. The more frequently this, or any other type of modification, is made in the instructional sequence to suit the needs of individual students, the greater is the degree of *individualization*. The way in which these changes are introduced is far less significant than the frequency and accuracy with which individual student needs are reflected in new decisions as to what each student should do next.

Self-instruction, or self-paced instruction, is not synonymous with individualized instruction. It is quite possible to give every student a programmed instruction (PI) text and tell him to go away to work on it, and return when he is ready to take the final examination. But if that's all that is done, the system has not come far along the continuum of individualization from conventional lecture programs. Such a program would not be individualized because the students all receive the same presentation regardless of their needs; no changes in the system occur to reflect individual performance. Other independent study programs, such as the audio-tutorial method or correspondence courses, are no more individualized than PI.

In this chapter we will explore the types of decisions teachers can make in *managing the instructional process* and their effect in terms of the degree and type of individualization provided. All observations and recommendations reflect the view that any procedure which enables the educational system to adapt itself more to an individual student's needs is more individualized.

INSTRUCTIONAL MANAGEMENT

Revolution in the quality of education will not come from the availability of new media or the introduction of any specific kinds of devices, like the computer or teaching machine, although all these will, in their way, contribute. Instead, it will come from the increased application of the growing body of knowledge about the form, purpose and processes involved in decision making in the classroom. The generally accepted term for this development is *instructional management*. Instructional management can be defined as *those activities involved in the decision to initiate a specific activity for a given student, based upon an assessment of that student's performance*. One of the most common examples of instructional management occurs when the instructor, ascertaining that a student is having difficulty learning a particular skill, decides to assign special homework or to provide individual tutoring. The general logic of this activity (i.e., *assessing performance* → *selecting presentation* → *initiating a new activity*) can be extended from this simple situation to provide the base for rules that can be used in a wide variety of circumstances.

TYPES OF INSTRUCTIONAL MANAGEMENT

There are essentially six types of instructional management procedures by which, singly or in combination, an instructor can make the system more responsive to individual student needs.

1. *Aspiration Management* determines the extent to which each student's goals will influence the learning steps he or she will pursue. Such goals may be long range or may reflect immediate interests. For example, the student who wants to be an engineer and therefore elects mathematics courses in high school is engaging in a form of aspiration self-management; so is the student whose sudden interest in ecology leads him to select a library book on the subject. Help in identifying such goals and finding ways to reflect them in the prescribed learning activities constitutes aspiration management. A free school can be considered the extreme in aspiration management. In such an educational environment, almost every decision reflects student interest.

2. *Achievement Management* controls the frequency and utility of the feedback given to students for remediation. This is by far the most frequently used form of instructional management but, at the same time, students often gain only a fraction of the utility it should provide. The problem is that to be useful, the feedback must reach the student at a time and in a form that will be used. Every test paper is an opportunity for a teacher to provide achievement management. But grades, or even graded test papers, serve little purpose if no provision is made for the student to attain the objectives he failed to master.

It is ironic to note that many of the teaching machines popular a few years ago gave the students the individual feedback but were so designed that the student was mechanically prevented from rereading the question he may have just missed.

Almost all individualized systems provide for some sort of progress check which is given after a student has completed an instructional activity. The purpose of the progress check is to determine if the student has acquired the information contained in that presentation. This check on mastery and the subsequent decisions for remediation defines another form of achievement management.

When it is determined that a student has failed to learn a particular unit of material, there can be two causes: 1) either the student did not attend to the information properly, or 2) he did not have the prerequisite knowledge to allow him to process the new information. Depending upon the manager's evaluation of the student's failure, there are three types of strategies the manager may use to remedy the achievement failure. These are:

Redundancy: The student may be asked to repeat the same or continue through many similar instructional presentations until he attains the objectives.

Multi-Form: The student may be asked to review the same information in a different instructional presentation form or via a different medium.

Multi-Level: The student may be asked to review the same information at a lower level of presentation (i.e., in a more expanded form using simpler vocabulary, syntax, etc.).

No matter how frequently the feedback occurs, it does not meet the criterion of utility unless it results in a change in the instructional sequence for each student depending on the performance observed.

3. *Prescriptive Management* provides students with well-informed decisions as to the *most efficient* learning activity for him as an individual (such decisions can often be made by the students themselves). The most frequently used form of prescriptive management involves the use of data from pre-tests to determine proper curriculum placement. This form of prescription allows the teacher to assign certain instructional units, exercises, or supplementary activities, based on knowledge of the materials available and of the learner's entry level skills. The efficiency occurs because the student can thus bypass large segments of instruction. Prescriptive management

strategies for curriculum placement vary in their complexities. The most elementary form can be seen in the "skip ahead if you know this material" options given in many programmed instruction courses.

A form of prescriptive management frequently proposed but seldom used in practice, is that which tries to offer different media or techniques in order to accommodate various learning styles. Proponents of such systems often make statements such as:

> "There are differences in learning styles. Some students learn better from pictorial presentations and others learn better from text. So, let us consider such differences in selecting the best instructional path for each student."

The general strategy for such forms of prescriptive management requires an analysis of each student's learning profile during previous instruction in order to predict the most appropriate instructional path for him. This "ideal path" would be designed to allow him to achieve the course objective in the most efficient manner possible.

In practice, however, a student's profile seldom provides the quantity or quality of information required for this type of prescriptive management. There is usually no practical alternative, therefore, but to give all students the same learning experience. If a student then has trouble with the standard path he may be given different, or additional, work to do. But this type of decision is clearly achievement management rather than prescriptive management. However, to obscure the fact that what is delivered is not what was promised, many existing programs refer to this as the "prescription."

Two quite different strategies of prescriptive management have been proposed for accommodating learning styles. The first of these may be called the iterative method. This strategy requires that a historical profile of student success be documented on specific instructional modules. Then the profiles of subsequent students are statistically matched to the historical profiles to predict the success of these new students on these specific modules. The new student is then given the best module for him selected from the available inventory of parallel modules. Because of the complexities of this strategy, the iterative method requires the use of a computer.

The second strategy may be called the *a priori* method. In this strategy individual characteristics of each student are used to predict that student's success in all instructional activities which use a particular presentation form or medium. For example, a poor reader may be given an audio-cassette version of the module.

The iterative strategy has so far proven to be the more practical approach. The historical profile for a given module of instruction is established from data on success-failure rates. This then allows one to define a student for whom this particular instructional module is ideal. Obviously, the strategy does not require an analytical description of the characteristics of the module since it is specific to the particular content, presentation form, and medium of that module.

In order for either strategy to be efficient, parallel instructional modules must be developed. These parallel modules must significantly fit various student profiles while reaching the same objectives. The resulting investment necessary to prepare alternative instructional paths must be justified in terms of possible increase in total system efficiency and effectiveness afforded by their use.

4. *Motivation Management* influences the intensity of the student's personal involvement in the learning process. No matter how good a learning system is, if the student becomes bored or stops working for any reason, the system will fail. One solution is to build motivational activities into instructional systems that ensure that the student's learning activities lead to a positive consequence. Such a concept is in perfect agreement with laboratory studies on reinforcement which typically use the positive consequence of eating or drinking to motivate behavior. These types of laboratory reinforcers are obviously not appropriate for the classroom but there are many other kinds of preferred activities that can be awarded in recognition of achievement.

One popular technique employed to increase motivation has

been termed "contingency management" which describes a systematic approach to ensure the availability of various kinds of rewards contingent on the satisfactory execution of each desired performance. In some programs, students agree in advance on contracts for rewards. For example, a student contract may state: "When you do your assignment and get 90% on the Progress Check Test, you may take a break." How the break time is used depends on the student's personal interests. Student contracts for reinforcing activities have been used in settings varying from preschool to college.

A variation of the contingency management approach is the establishment of a token economy, or micro-economy. In such systems, satisfactory performance leads to the deliverance of points or tokens which can later be used to buy desirable objects or activities. A technique often used both at the secondary and college levels is to give grades on the basis of a cumulative number of points earned by taking tests and/or working on a project. Such systems are special cases of a micro-economy strategy. The awarding of the points is immediate, even though the grade may be a long time in coming.

Many individualized systems that employ some form of achievement management impose a mastery contingency—the student must achieve 90% of the objectives of one section before he is given a "reward" and allowed to progress to the next. When properly handled in the classroom, this technique establishes a strong motivational contingency. It is interesting to speculate that while most proponents of individualized instruction emphasize the prescriptive and remedial decisions made in their programs, it is quite possible that the motivational management component introduced by the mastery contingency is the most important factor in the success of such programs.

5. *Enrichment Management* broadens the students' ability to identify applications, in their own personal experience, of concepts learned. This often involves the selection of materials that are related

to the basic core content but which either go into more depth or present interesting sidelights into core concepts. Some reasons given for enrichment management are that it acts as a time filler, aids in motivating the student, provides for wider application of principles learned, and so on. This type of instructional management is becoming more effective as systems become more refined. At this stage of systems development, however, it usually exists not by plan but because system objectives are so vague that instructors are uncertain whether or not a particular segment of material is necessary to the achievement of a particular set of learning objectives. (See Chapter 12.)

6. *Maintenance Management* influences the extent to which the student will be able to recall important information or continue to maintain a skill after the initial learning experience. Techniques can be used while the course is in progress to improve the student's retention of skills acquired early in the course.

A procedure called Comprehensive Achievement Monitoring (CAM) has been developed by W. P. Gorth and P. Schriever, University of Massachusetts, and Robert O'Reilly, New York Education Department. In this system, one year's work in a subject area (such as elementary arithmetic) is specified in terms of a series of objectives. Parallel test batteries are then prepared to measure student performance on these objectives. Students are given a complete battery at regular intervals throughout the year and data on individual student achievement is then given to the teacher. By this procedure the CAM may reveal a performance loss over a period of time, which would require that the student be assigned additional review exercises (maintenance management).

This program has been implemented on a limited basis within the New York State Education System. Success to date has led the State to expand the program to include reading.

RECOMMENDATIONS

Individualized instruction is typically defined in terms of the resources employed, e.g., the integrated use of media, the use of proctors, self-paced materials, the requirement of mastery learning, and so on.

We find it much more useful to the instructor to define individualized instruction in terms of its impact on the learner, specifically in terms of the frequency and quality of the decisions to change instructional presentations as a result of assessing student performance. This approach provides a taxonomy of *strategies* which can be used to accomplish individualization.

It is not necessary in this chapter to describe detailed procedures within all of these categories. On these matters, teachers are already well informed. We recommend, however, that every procedure employed in the classroom can and should be evaluated in terms of its effects within these six types of instructional management. Once this is done, the instructor can assess more objectively the management decisions made from day to day and make more deliberate changes in his or her classroom procedures to strengthen one *type* of instructional management at a time.

5

Media Employed In Instructional Management

One of the more hotly debated issues in education is the student-teacher ratio. It is generally agreed that a reduction in this ratio will be accompanied by an increase in teaching effectiveness, a view which has so much surface logic that it seems to be accepted usually without question. The controversy isn't over whether a reduction in the ratio is desirable, but over how much of a reduction is possible within the limits of the budget. Unfortunately, this controversy is so overpowering that it often seems to blot out consideration of other changes that could be equally useful in improving educational effectiveness.

The time and effort spent arguing about student-teacher ratios is unfortunate, both because the arguments are futile and because they are diversionary.

- They are futile because there is no chance that education on a large scale can afford a student-teacher ratio low enough for any further reductions to have any impact on teaching effectiveness. There is convincing evidence now that in conventional group-paced instruction, changes in class size influence learning only when the class has fifteen or less students; learning effectiveness in a class with more than twenty students is not influenced much if the number is raised to thirty or to three hundred. Since most of the arguments take place about class sizes in excess of thirty, the time spent in these arguments has very little effect on the students, no matter who wins.
- The arguments are diversionary because, by focusing so much emotion on the question of how many students a teacher should

handle, they cloud the more critical issue — that is, *what the teacher is able to do differently in managing the student's learning environment to make it more responsive to his needs*. The phrase "Give more personal attention" is not an adequate explanation of the changes that take place when class sizes are reduced to less than fifteen students.

In this chapter, we will ignore the question of class size itself, that being the type of solution that no large school system can afford, and concentrate directly on the instructional management strategies which bring the benefit to the students regardless of whether they are achieved by lower class size or by some other means. The question is one of finding ways to introduce instructional management procedures in such a way that students can gain the same benefits they might achieve in far smaller classes.

When students get more personal attention, they tend to learn better; not because they're getting *more tutoring*, but because they're getting *better guidance*. That is, personal attention does not usually result in more detailed explanations of the subject matter to each student, but instead, as teachers become more intimately aware of each student's progress and problems, they are able to give each student *more frequent and better-informed advice* as to what he or she should do next. Anything that increases the ability of the teacher to concentrate on important judgments of this type will benefit the student. Reducing the number of students is one way to accomplish this objective, but not the only one. A far more practicable approach is to relieve the teacher of the workload associated with other tasks that do not require the special skills that only the teacher possesses.

COMPONENTS OF THE INSTRUCTIONAL RESPONSIBILITY

In general the teacher's responsibilities fall into three areas:

1. *Preparation*. This includes selecting all study materials to be

used in the course, organizing the presentation of the material, planning the students' activities through the course and deciding how student progress will be monitored and evaluated.

2. *Administration*. The responsibility includes presenting (or arranging for the presentation of) the learning experience, monitoring and recording the students' progress, and making the final evaluation of the students' achievement.

3. *Instructional Management*. This activity — taking a meaningful part in the guidance of students — is perceived by most teachers as their most important and satisfying role.

There are three distinct functions that must be performed for instructional management and there are a variety of devices (media) that may be employed in the execution of these functions. The functions are:

1. *Assessment*, which involves the acquisition and processing of data about student performance, and the arrangement of that information in a form from which valid judgments can be made.

2. *Decision*, which involves using the assessed data to make day-to-day decisions regarding individual student assignments. Such decisions range from those that can be accomplished according to pre-established rules (e.g., if a student misses question 28 he should re-study Chapter 4) to those that require the expert judgment of an experienced teacher (e.g., determining if a student needs more practice in pronouncing the Spanish vowels).

3. *Initiation*, those devices that activate the assigned learning experiences. This is the simplest function, and the one which can most easily be delegated by the teacher to an aide or to the student himself.

If the teacher is the only medium available to carry out all of the above responsibilities, there obviously has to be some limit on the number of students one teacher can handle effectively. The teacher is a flexible and potent management medium, but giving individual assignments to each of thirty students within normal classroom constraints usually isn't practical. This difficulty can be mitigated by the introduction of new display media which free the instructor from some of the time-consuming tasks of dispensing information, thus giving him more time for the decision-making aspects of the instructional management role. Recent trends toward differentiated staffing can also be used to reduce the burden by allowing teacher aides or paraprofessionals to perform some of the supporting activities.

Different display media and differentiated staffing can often save the teacher a good deal of time. The important instructional management decisions, however, involve a reduction in the extent to which the teacher is used as the medium for carrying out the functions of preparation, administration, and advice described above. The most frequently used alternative media are:

- Computers
- Proctors
- The students themselves

Computer Management

In varying degrees, depending on the subject matter and circumstances, computers can partially substitute for the instructor within the management function. In the most limited case, the computer is used only for assessment, e.g., grading and summarizing results. The instructor still makes the assignment decisions and initiates all new activities.

Instructors who have used such systems recognize that there is no magic in the computer. Certainly it can process data more rapidly, with greater accuracy, and often at less cost than people can. But its decision-making function is far less complex and far more costly than that of a teacher. Any teacher or proctor can usually follow most of the same decision rules that are built into computer-aided instruction, at much less cost. Thus, computers are typically used only for the data processing function.

On the other hand, there are strong arguments for computer *managed* instruction (as opposed to computer *aided* instruction) in which some of the simpler decision rules are programmed directly into the computer. In this application, the computer not only processes data regarding the student's performance, it also selects from a range of simple alternatives the best assignment to be pursued next. In fact, for some purposes, the students' interactions can be directly with the computer, even to the extent of receiving the written description of the next assignment.

In evaluations of the Project PLAN classrooms (described in Chapter 16) it was found that students performed better when they were able to interact *directly* with the computer. It appeared that the necessity for the students to feed the computer and respond to its output kept the instructional sequence on the track. This had a beneficial effect on the classroom behavior of both teachers and students.

Proctor Management

Although the computer has stirred the greatest and most controversial interest, it certainly is not the only non-teacher management medium that can be used. By far the most widely used of these media are teacher aides or proctors. The proctors are usually older and more advanced students, but sometimes they are selected from the students in the class itself.

In such systems, the aides are used primarily as assessors, but they sometimes give tests, become involved in the decision function and, less frequently, act as initiators. Dr. Fred Keller, a leading proponent of proctor-managed instruction, finds that the principal advantages in using proctors are: an opportunity for repeated testing, immediate scoring, almost unavoidable tutoring, and a marked enhancement of the personal-social aspect of the educational process.

Most of the teachers who use this system emphasize the personal aspects of the student-proctor interaction. There is no evidence, however, that a less personal management medium produces any significant changes either in student motivation or in learning.

Student Management

In any interactions between a student and a tutor, a student and a computer, or a student and a proctor, there are at least two devices capable of evaluating data and making decisions, one of which is the student himself. It is becoming much more popular to make use of the fact that the student can assess much of the data on his own performance and make the simpler types of decisions against established decision rules. These decisions may require only minimal guidance. For example, when a student views a presentation and makes a response which is assessed by a computer, there are at least two options available. The computer can make the decision to assign the student to an appropriate learning sequence, or it can simply provide the student with the assessed data and allow him to select the next learning sequence himself. In a study of a CAI project at the U.S. Naval Academy, it was estimated that perhaps 80% of all student errors could be remedied merely by having the student re-examine the original presentation.

One of the reasons for the growing popularity of using the student as an instructional management medium is that it tends to make the student more responsible for correcting his own errors. Getting the student more involved in his own learning process not only reduces many logistic and cost problems but it builds in habits of independent learning which most people agree should be encouraged. Observations of two-year college students in an individualized program indicated that self-management was the most significant factor in student success.

RECOMMENDATIONS

Each of these instructional management media — the teacher, the computer, the proctor, and the student himself — has advantages and limitations. The instructional system designer's problem is to develop a total system that will incorporate the best mix of these management media.

We believe that the most neglected medium is the student himself. Accordingly, we recommend that more emphasis be put on student self-management, with teacher assistance. In larger classes, some form of proctor or computer management is essential.

6

Converting Programmed Instruction And Audio-Tutorial Programs To Individualized Systems

During the last ten years, the idea of independent study programs has achieved widespread popularity. Most colleges and many high schools now operate such programs. Generally such programs are designed with one or more of four objectives in mind:

1. To reward students who are already doing well in their regular courses. A student who has performed well and is confident of his or her ability to work alone enjoys the freedom from class attendance and periodic deadlines. We are not aware, however, of any evidence that the prospect of earning independent study privileges has influenced the classroom performance of students who are not already performing at a high level.

2. To instill greater self-motivation in the student. A student who achieves the course objectives without supervised instruction is presumed to have acquired an ability to motivate himself. As already noted, however, such privileges are seldom awarded to students whose motivation has not been demonstrated already.

3. To provide better utilization of instructional resources. The logic

for this objective is sound, in that fewer resources are required if they don't have to be used by large groups all at once. Little impact has been felt in this area, however, because the number of students admitted to independent study is a very small percent of the total.

4. To provide remediation for students who enter without prerequisite skills to enable them to compete successfully in a group-paced class.

While the independent study programs have not achieved all their original objectives, they were instrumental in establishing a widespread acquaintance with new instructional techniques. The two most popular techniques used in independent study programs to date are programmed instruction methods and the audio-tutorial approach, both of which are now being used to implement more individualized classroom procedures.

Programmed instruction was first introduced in the early 1960's and there are now several thousand commercially available programmed instruction courses covering a wide spectrum of academic and occupational areas at many levels. The audio-tutorial method is a more recent development. It originated with Dr. Postlethwait at Purdue University, who was originally interested in simply providing a means by which students who missed lectures could make them up by listening to recordings. The original method has since evolved into a sophisticated instructional system and the make up feature is now of little or no importance in the overall program.

Even more recently, instructors employed these techniques, originally used for independent study programs outside the classroom, to provide for greater individualization in regular classroom instruction. In pursuing this goal, however, many have erroneously concluded that, because independent study programs allow students to proceed more at their own pace, such programs also provide for greater individualization. In fact, most independent study programs are no more individualized than are conventional group-paced instruction or correspondence courses.

The individualization process requires that some means be provided to assess each student's needs and interests and make individual assignments to students as a result of those assessments. The frequency with which this activity is performed determines the degree of individualization. The *techniques* of independent study do not necessarily result in individual decisions for individual students; it is necessary to modify the procedures by which those techniques are used.

INDIVIDUALIZING PROGRAMMED INSTRUCTION

Most programmed instruction workbooks are tested and validated to ensure that students who complete all the frames achieve the learning objectives. Hence the requirement to monitor performance frequently for purposes of providing remedial assignments (achievement management) is not the principal problem with programmed instruction. Motivational and prescriptive problems are usually the ones requiring special attention.

Strategies for Motivational Management

Motivation problems are often encountered with programmed instruction because of the tedium caused by the large number of responses demanded of the student. The usual solution to this problem is to make the programmed instruction text mandatory; just force the student through it whether he likes it or not. There are alternatives, however. Many instructors are using some form of motivational management to reduce the boredom that is almost always associated with programmed instruction.

The typical programmed course of a few years ago contained 2000 frames in a linear sequence without even chapter breaks to indicate where students might conveniently stop for the day. Programmed instruction was often touted as being intrinsically motivating, because the small steps supposedly gave the student frequent feelings of success. In fact, the small steps often produced the opposite effect. The student was never sure when he had mastered a concept because the process seemed endless. The perception of mastery was often even further blurred by the introduction of review sequences. It seemed to many students that "old" questions never died and only seldom faded away.

Today most programmed instruction courses at least provide for convenient break points at intervals of approximately 50 to 60 frames. Many users have taken advantage of these break points to introduce a short test or progress check. The progress check has two beneficial aspects. It permits the student to demonstrate the progress achieved at each point; and it provides a frequent opportunity to reward the student for his accomplishments. This second feature, the opportunity to provide rewards, has led to the development of a number of motivational strategies, most of which are extensions of contingency management. In these contingency managed systems, students often contract that they will complete a segment of instructional materials and achieve a certain percentage on progress checks in order to earn the opportunity to participate in various types of rewarding activities.

A typical contract might be expressed as follows: A student will complete 50 frames and take a progress check test. If he scores 90% or above, he will earn a 15 minute break. If the score is less than 90% he will proceed through a remedial path as indicated by the instructor. After completing this assignment he may take a parallel form of the progress check test to earn the break. Depending on the circumstances, the rewards provided may simply be: taking a break, shooting a game of pool, talking to a fellow student, having a cigarette, playing a card game, and so on. Similar procedures have been used at all levels of education ranging from pre-school to college, the differences being in the selection of the activities that the students find rewarding.

Strategies for Prescriptive Management

A second way to achieve an individualized effect with programmed instruction is to introduce some form of prescriptive management. The fact is that not all students need all the drill-and-practice routines that programmed instruction texts provide. Any teacher who has used programmed instruction can testify that many students could have proceeded through the program at a faster rate if they had been allowed to skip the more elementary sections of the text.

Prescription provided by means of a pre-test is often an answer. Such tests allow the instructor to assign instructional exercises tailored to each learner. Usually the pre-test is used to survey the existing skill areas or repertoires of the learner. Such tests divide the subject matter competence into many sub-areas or steps according to skills needed to go from entry levels to the terminal objectives of the course. The outcome of prescriptive pre-tests may be related directly to a curriculum decision or may indicate the need for more precise testing. Flow charts may be employed as a device to aid the instructor in making accurate prescriptions.

Another tactic for prescriptive management employs the student himself as the instructional manager. This involves giving the student a choice of the conventional route through the course, or a fast track. The fast track is devised by the instructor by first determining what frames represent essential criterion performance and those designed merely to introduce and lead up to the concept. The criterion frames and perhaps a few of their introductory frames are then listed as the fast track. The more able student may elect to work only those frames which cover all the important points but skip over the detailed development. When the fast track prescription is provided it must be used in conjunction with progress check tests to assure achievement of the prescribed learning objectives.

INDIVIDUALIZING AUDIO-TUTORIAL INSTRUCTION

In the audio-tutorial method, the audio-tapes not only provide the primary source of instruction but also act as the major organizational device for the course. Some activities do not lend themselves to presentation on tape and need to be provided by other means (e.g., guest lecturers, films, or oral discussions with other students) but the tape directs the student to such activities. There are typically four types of learning experiences used in audio-tutorial programs.

1. *General Assembly Session (GAS)*
All students meet in a large group session one hour each week. Activities include receiving general directions, announcements, watching movies, listening to guest lecturers, and so forth. *Purpose*: To orient the student to relationships between the subject matter and the various learning activities he will be engaged in.

2. *Home Study Session (HSS)*
Activities include reading texts, outside reprints, etc. *Purpose*: To provide experience in obtaining additional sources of information.

3. *Independent Study Session(ISS)*
These sessions focus on the audio-tutorial booth in a learning center. Tutors are on duty to provide special assistance. The learning center is usually operated on an open or unscheduled basis, so that students may enter at their own convenience and remain as long as necessary. *Purpose*: To provide the primary learning vehicle for the course content and to provide for increased student interaction with the educational materials provided.

4. *Integrated Quiz Session (IQS)*
Informal group discussion with eight to ten students and an instructor or aide. Students are picked at random by the instructor to respond to questions about material studied in the independent study session. *Purpose*: To act as a progress check on performance in the independent study session. Instructors may use this session to provide for limited motivational and achievement management. The instructor

may identify students who are falling behind or who need special assistance. Also, since the points for grades are contingent upon performance in the integrated quiz session, a degree of motivational management is provided. (Note: Both these activities are usually done in a relatively informal way.)

The following diagram is a sample of the "flow" of a typical audio-tutorial program.

In its usual form an audio-tutorial program consists of both group and independent learning activities, and provides a test to evaluate student accomplishment. Each student receives essentially the same learning task, and the data on student achievement is *not* used to take any differential action, but only to give a grade (presumably to motivate students).

Unlike programmed instruction, audio-tutorial programs generally are not validated, hence there is more need for procedures to verify that learning has occurred. The following diagram indicates a possible strategy for accomplishing the necessary achievement management condition:

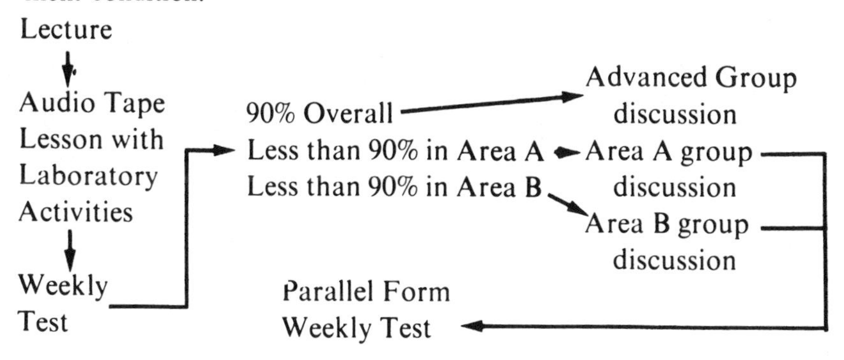

Note: Individualization via achievement management has been added by using the weekly test as a diagnostic aid and by providing alternative discussion groups for remediation.

RECOMMENDATIONS

We have discussed three types of instructional management strategies which may be used with independent study systems to make them more responsive to student needs:

1. Provide for pre-testing to allow more able students to bypass the less important portions of an instructional system (prescriptive management).

2. Provide for post-testing to allow for remediation (achievement management).

3. Provide incentives for successful completion of the learning activities (motivational management).

These same procedures, however, have broad applicability and we recommend that these procedures be considered not only for programmed instruction and audio-tutorial methods, but for many other forms of instruction as well.

7

Selecting The Most Appropriate Display Media

According to Webster, a medium is "a means of effecting or conveying something." Since in education we are obviously concerned with conveying information and effecting learning, it should follow that the selection of media should be a significant decision. But, to date, research into media effects has yielded few practical results. It could be, as some researchers have pointed out, that the fault lies in the quality of the experimentation we conduct in media research. Or, on the other hand, it may be that *media effects in themselves are not significant enough in the teaching-learning process to warrant investigation.*

Hardware salesmen are pleased to report on the success of the latest computerized gizmo. Even defense of the traditional media of lecture, laboratory, and text is voiced. However, when the extant literature is examined from a standpoint of what is actually known about the learning process, ineligible data, faulty generalizations and appeals to the emotions or artistic inclinations are apparent. If procedures for learning are to be improved at a reasonable pace, then a more dispassionate approach to media selection is necessary.

Unfortunately, emotion almost always plays a part in media selection. A particular medium may have an aura of advantage surrounding it. It is multisensory...it is new...it has been successfully used in other settings...or it has received great press reviews. The novice designer may, therefore, inappropriately select this medium because of its supposed intrinsic advantages which unfortunately are too often not relevant to what he is trying to teach.

It would be nice if one could counter the claims of a media "fan" with hard research data. But, as we pointed out previously, most media studies report no significant differences among media. Even Confucius' claim that "a picture is worth a thousand words" has not been supported by research. Allen (1960), in his very comprehensive analysis of media research, concluded that very little evidence has been reported on the educational value of pictorial illustrations; and what little there is, is contradictory.

The truth of the matter is that almost anything can be taught with almost any medium. The media mix of a lecturer and a blackboard does teach (we were all educated that way). The successes of home study courses and programmed instruction indicate that the printed word with illustrations can do a fair job of instruction. Of course these successes do not mean that such systems represent either the most effective or the most efficient media mix possible.

Recent attempts to bring order to the question of media selection have drawn on the work of the behaviorists who conclude that the quality of an educational system must be evaluated in terms of its ability to modify either directly or indirectly the behavior of the student. To demonstrate that learning has occurred it must be possible to show that the student can *say*, or *write*, or *do something new*. Understanding cannot be verified by looking into the student's mind.

In designing a behavioral change system, several classes of variables must be considered (see Figure 1).

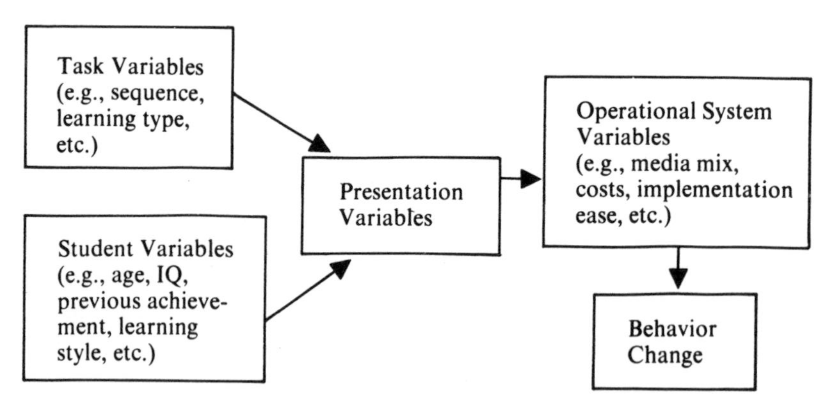

Figure 1. Classes of Variables

The criterion for choosing display media can be stated simply as: Decide what to teach (what are the behavioral objectives) and then select a media mix which is within your present resources and which does not severely limit the effectiveness of the presentation.

It may sound backwards to suggest choosing a medium, not on its advantages, but on an analysis of its limitations. But, as previously pointed out, almost anything can be taught with almost any medium. The point can be illustrated with an analogy from engineering. Civil engineers have analyzed all the available building materials (media) to determine their breaking point. When they design a structure, they select the most cost-effective materials and then compensate for the limitations inherent in this material either by overdesign (i.e., using more of the same type of material) or by mixing other materials within the structure.

A similar approach can be used in designing educational programs: first define the limitations of the various media available, then select the most cost-effective medium that will do the job. Finally, supplement it with other media to overcome any limitations that may be inherent in the primary medium. The final choice of media depends on the presentation requirements. If visual illustration is needed, then audio-tape cannot meet the requirements; but an illustrated book, film strip, or overhead transparency will do an adequate job.

ATTRIBUTES OF DISPLAY MEDIA

Before we can do an analysis of media we must have some way of classifying those important attributes so that we can make intelligent comparisons. There are more than 100 variables which have been identified in selecting media. We can categorize the most significant of these into two groupings: *stimulus forms* and *durational considerations*.

Stimulus Forms

Stimulus forms are obvious attributes of every presentation. Man has invented many specialized forms for encoding information. Some forms (language, for example) enable him to convey data about the real world without the necessity of having objects available, while others (mathematics) allow him to condense or summarize data. Still others (Morse code) are designed to allow more rapid delivery of information and to reduce the cost of information transmission.

Although there are many ways in which information can be displayed, the more important forms can be categorized as:

1. *Environmental structure*. Real three-dimensional objects may be used as educational media either alone or in certain combinations. An example of this occurs when a student examines a flower or counts a row of blocks. Often the medium employed for the environmental structure allows the student to utilize a combination of senses. He can see it, feel it, smell it, taste it, and/or hear it. Some educators, particularly those using the Montessori approach, place a great deal of emphasis on this aspect of environmental stimuli. There are, however, conflicting data which indicate that a multiplicity of sensory events is not necessarily superior to one sensation alone. The decision to introduce a medium which demands that the student use more than one sense should depend on the behavioral objectives.

2. *Pictorial*. Pictorial encoding requires a reproduction of either real or imagined visual aspects of objects. Photographs can reproduce a scene with great fidelity. Some media used for pictorial presentation, such as paintings and illustrations, eliminate or exaggerate various parts of an object.

3. *Symbolic*. Man has created many stimuli which stand for other stimuli which may be more complex, less abstract, or more difficult to manipulate. (A very important class of such symbols is the verbals, which are considered separately below.) Symbols range from graphics to schematics, and from numerals to equations. Most sym-

bolic encoding is in the visual dimension; but some, such as that delivered by fire sirens, is aural.

4. *Verbal*. Words and verbal syntax are the stimuli of the verbal encoding form. These may be either aural or visual. Some of the media most often employed to carry verbal presentations are humans (lectures) and books (prose).

DURATION

Duration refers to the length of time the display remains unchanged. Presentations vary from transient to persistent. Books are very persistent media (the reader can spend as much time as he wishes before he turns the page). On the other hand, the presentation conveyed by motion pictures is usually very transient. The characteristic of duration is very important in media selection.

Limitations of Transient Media

The primary disadvantage of transient presentations is that the information just presented often puts an enormous load on the student's memory since the images or words are gone shortly after the initial presentation. The requirement for the student to store information places limits on the ability of media employing a transient presentation to generate new learning, particularly if the tasks involve highly complex information.

Often the teacher might wish to select a highly transient presentation because it more nearly reproduces the real life situation. But even in this case, it may still be preferable to use a more persistent medium such as a workbook. Often an exact simulation of the "real life" situation is too rapid to allow the student to follow all the steps in a complicated sequence. We certainly wouldn't expect a student to grasp all the techniques of carburetor repair by seeing a motion picture of a mechanic doing the repair at a real time pace. Often by going to a more persistent presentation, the action can be stopped, and the operation can be simplified to isolate those particular points to which the student should attend.

Limitations of Persistent Media

As implied in the previous paragraph, a disadvantage of persistent media is the inability to show the real time steps in a sequence. In some cases, this has been overcome by employing cues to indicate time or motion. Illustrations, such as showing arrows or providing a fixed sequential pattern as in comic books, do help. But even with these substitutes, students can't really feel the time constraints that may be imposed.

Another way to overcome disadvantages of persistent media is to combine persistent with more transient presentations. The lecture and blackboard is the most common example of this media mix. In teaching a sequence of operations such as in welding, we have found it best to strengthen the individual behaviors with a persistent presentation as in a PI workbook, then follow this presentation with a transient one displayed by a slide-tape device which better simulates the real life situation.

The Media Chart

To aid in visualizing the kinds of trade-offs that are possible, Figure 2 shows a chart of media in terms of the stimulus and duration properties. Many media appear in several places, since several encoding forms can be carried by those media. For example, flash cards can have words or equations on them, texts may display pictorial and verbal presentations, and sound motion pictures usually convey both pictorial and verbal presentations simultaneously.

Often there is no one best medium or media mix for a given behavioral objective. In this case, the final selection between media should be based on other constraints such as:

1. *Cost*. This includes developmental costs, purchase costs of media devices, initial set-up costs, and the cost of maintaining the system.

2. *Availability of various media*, e.g., tutors, audiovisual devices, etc.

3. *Market or user preference.*

PROCEDURE FOR SELECTING A MEDIUM

The following six steps denote a first approximation of a practical scheme for selecting media.

1. Establish the behavioral objectives.

2. Derive the stimulus forms and duration considerations from the objectives. List these on one axis of the media chart.

3. List the available media choices on the other axis.

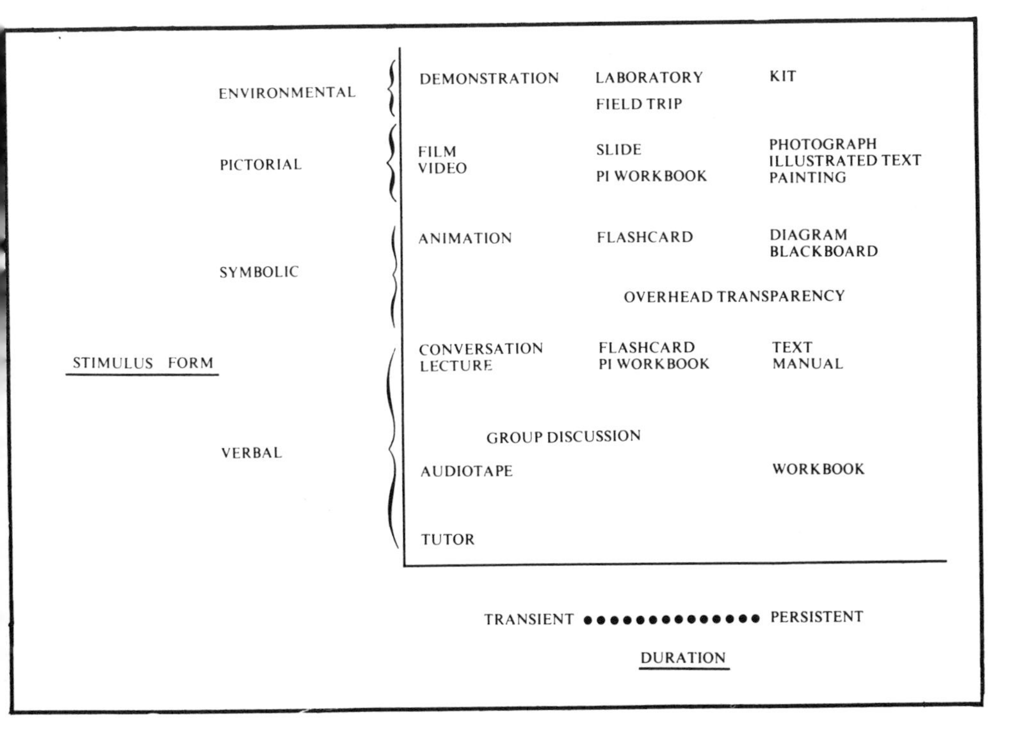

Figure 2. Media Classified by Stimulus Form Versus Duration

4. Select one or more media and indicate their limitations.
5. Revise the media list based on external constraints.
6. Select a medium from the remaining choices in the media list.

Working through an example will clarify the procedure. Consider the following objective statement:

> Given a coin minted by the British Empire during the period 1200 AD-1400 AD, the student will be able to name and characterize the purpose or origin of each mark on the coin.

Since the marks on the coin must be seen to be identified, a picture is necessary. In addition the student is to be able to identify the purpose of each mark, so this information must also be provided. Therefore the pictorial presentation should be supplemented by a verbal form. The duration could be toward the transient end of the scale since the amount of detail on the coin is small. A tabulation of these choices may appear as follows:

Stimulus form ....pictorial and vocal
Duration ....momentary

Now a decision table can be constructed listing the required presentation form along the left side and the media choices along the top as shown in Figure 3. Then the boxes can be filled in with checks or scaled numbers representing the applicability of each medium choice to each presentation form.

PRESENTATION FORM	MEDIA		
	Film	Book	Audio-tape
Symbolic	✓	✓	NO
Vocal	✓	✓	X
Momentary	✓	NO	X

Of the media choices listed, only film meets all of the requirements. But now we must consider the external constraints that might be applied. Figure 4 shows a number of these constraints.

CONSTRAINTS	MEDIA		
	Film	Book	Audio- tape
Cost	$4.00 per student	$.75 per student	$1.10 per student
Availability	good	good	poor
Ease of Individualized Student Use	poor	good	fair

Figure 4.

In this case, for example, the budget may not accommodate the cost of film, in which case the book would be the natural choice. However, a book has limits in the display of a momentary presentation. Thus, combining a book with an audio-tape presentation might compensate for this deficiency. The resulting media mix, although not as desirable from a learning standpoint as the original choice of films, may well suffice, and one can be confident that the best media have been selected within the existing constraints of cost.

RECOMMENDATIONS

We are still far short of a technology for media selection. Unfortunately neither the research data nor appeals to emotion aid much in the choice. We have attempted in this chapter to present a practical method of selection developed from:

1. Knowledge of what one wishes to teach.
2. The nature of the media limitations.
3. System constraints.

4. Possible trade-offs.

Following the procedure we have outlined should at least prevent anyone from making drastic errors and eliminate the specter of useless devices gathering dust in a corner.

8

Operating A Proctor-Managed System

Increased pressures of cost have led to the increased utilization of lower paid assistants to perform some of the simpler tasks that would otherwise have to be carried out by the instructor. These may range from volunteer mothers helping to keep order in elementary school classes, to advanced students hired on an hourly basis to grade papers, to highly-qualified teaching assistants at the college and university level.

The move toward differentiated staffing may reduce the load on the teachers and provide closer supervision of student behavior in the classroom. However, unless this assistance is used in a way that effects a change in instructional management procedures, there is no evidence from which to conclude that it has any influence on student learning.

Breaking a large lecture class of 300 down into ten groups of thirty, each under the direction of a teaching assistant, does little for the students if the teaching assistant only does the same thing that the lecturer does in a lecture hall. Volunteer mothers can be extremely helpful in the lower grades if they are given useful work to do, i.e., if they are given an opportunity to respond at least to some of the simpler learning needs of each student.

There is a growing number of teachers who have come to the conclusion that the traditional roles have had little effect on student achievement. It is this recognition that has led to the development of a proctor-managed system.

CHARACTERISTICS OF A PROCTOR-MANAGED SYSTEM

There are several critical points of difference that distinguish a proctor-managed system (as outlined in this chapter) from the traditional teaching assistance approach:

- The instructional system itself differs from the traditional group-paced classroom approach in which the teacher is the only one who has any authority to make decisions regarding the activities of the students.
- The injection of a proctor into the system is not just an add-on; the proctor's role changes the roles of both the students and the teachers.
- The proctors are not tutors; that is, they do not teach the course in the sense of presenting materials to the student. Generally they have a defined scope of authority to evaluate student performance and to indicate to each student his or her next assignment based on that evaluation.
- Their role is not to assist the teacher but to be of direct assistance to individual students. Proctors play a supporting role by providing a degree of interaction with individual students that is not possible in conventional lecture instruction.

Proctors can be extremely valuable in increasing individual student achievement. This value is only realized, however, when the system within which a proctor is working meets the criteria defined above.

Getting value from proctors requires a well-defined understanding of what they are to do. An example of a situation in which this is not done is illustrated by the use of proctors in an audiovisual center. The example we have in mind is an extremely expensively-equipped center in California in which students have access at all times of day to a wide range of material on film and tape which can be played as often as needed on equipment provided in study carrels. A proctor is on duty at all times to assist students but the fact is that there has been no *systematic* provision made for any interaction with individual students at specified points in their learning sequence. In effect, the proctor acts as low-grade librarian making sure the reels are put back in the proper place and generally keeping the center neat and orderly.

The essential requirement for the successful operation of a proctor-managed system is a formal procedure that gives the proctor some meaningful segment of the instructional system to manage. Just assisting the teacher, while admittedly a desirable condition in itself, does not necessarily contribute any significant value to a student. Assuming, however, that a teacher does wish to establish a proctor function according to these guidelines, there is now enough successful experience with the system to enable one to plan and implement it with considerable confidence that it will succeed. The key steps in the implementation process are the selection and orientation of the proctors and a careful definition of the guidelines and procedures within which they will operate.

SELECTION AND ORIENTATION

Generally a proctor is an advanced student in the course being taught, a student who has recently completed the course, or a graduate student specializing in the subject matter of the course. While it is not up to the proctor to actually teach the course, presentation of material not being one of his responsibilities, he will be expected to evaluate certain aspects of student performance and reach conclusions as to what each student's next learning activity should be. This role requires some knowledge of the subject matter, although the extent of that knowledge will be determined, in part, by the nature and quality of the learning materials used in the course, as well as the extent to which the student is expected to master learning objectives not covered in the course material itself. If, for example the required learning objectives are covered in the course material and course tests are accompanied with answer keys indicating the material that should be restudied for each question that is missed, the degree of subject matter expertise required of the proctor is relatively small. On the other hand, if the student is expected to master topics that are only covered in discussion or lectures and the proctor is given no specific guidance in analyzing student responses, the requirement for subject matter expertise may be very high. These types of considerations must influence the identification of sources from which to select proctor candidates.

As a general guideline, one proctor can work effectively with about fifteen students and an instructor can work effectively with about ten proctors. In classes with more than 150 students, instructors sometimes establish a role of supervising proctor—usually someone with a higher order of subject matter expertise — working with every group of ten proctors. The supervising proctor then works with the instructor in monitoring the activities of the proctors.

In some cases each proctor is assigned, at the beginning of the term, to work with a single group of students (fifteen or less) and he works with the same group throughout the term. In other cases proctors are assigned duty hours and are available to work with any student who is ready for evaluation and assignment during these times. As long as the students know when they need to have a proctor evaluation, either system seems to work about equally well.

The proctors should be interviewed and selections made with enough time before the course begins to enable the instructor to make sure they know what they will be doing from the very first day. This is an extremely important requirement because, especially in an individualized course, the most critical period of the term for the student is the first two weeks. In fact, proctors are often advised that one of their most important responsibilities will be to make sure each student experiences a sense of achievement during that first two week period. The attitude toward the course and the study habits developed during this period are extremely difficult to change later on, and a student's overall achievement in the course depends, perhaps more than anything else, on the way his instruction is managed at the very beginning.

Other items that should be included in the initial proctor orientation sessions before the term begins are:

- A clear definition of the course content and scope and an acquaintance with the sources of materials or other activities from which the students will draw in achieving the learning objectives.
- The specific responsibilities of the proctor, i.e., the number of students with whom he will work and the procedural basis of the interactions.
- The incentives that are provided for participation as proctors. These may include wages or perhaps course credit.
- The number of hours that will be required per week in each activity, e.g., preparation, student interaction, administrative or follow-up orientation with other proctors and the instructor.

HOW INTERACTIONS ARE HANDLED

In most proctor-managed systems, there is a sequence of steps which defines exactly the point at which a student and proctor must meet for evaluation and assignment. With only minor modification, these steps can be described as follows:

1. A student works through a given segment of learning material on his own; usually requiring no more than a week of independent study.

2. The student obtains a test from the proctor covering the portion of the material that has just been studied.

3. The student completes the test either alone or under the proctor's supervision, depending on the nature of the test.

4. The proctor evaluates the student's performance immediately and gives him feedback on the spot. This is one of the most important advantages of a proctor-managed system. Feedback that reaches the student weeks or even days after he has completed the test has almost no effect on his performance in the future.

5. Depending on whether the performance was at the required level the proctor may certify that the objective has been achieved and assign a new unit of material to be covered or give the student selected remedial assignments.

6. If the student is progressing rapidly through the course and demonstrates a particular interest in some special aspect of the subject matter, the proctor may also suggest alternative enrichment activities.

This is a fairly typical description of the basic elements of the proctor's role with the student. He may also conduct additional counseling sessions with individual students and he would also be expected to keep progress records so that he could initiate special sessions with any student who appears to be falling behind.

RESPONSIBILITIES OF THE INSTRUCTOR

Clearly it is up to the instructor to define the limits within which the proctors have authority to make decisions about student activities. The instructor always retains the authority in defining the grading criteria applied by the proctors in their evaluations of student performance and for designing and scheduling the ways in which learning materials will be presented to the student. The quality of the student's learning experiences is the responsibility of the instructor and is never delegated to anyone else.

The instructor maintains whatever checks he considers necessary on the performance of the proctors by working occasionally with individual students in the various activities usually performed by the proctor and by meeting periodically with the proctors to discuss the performance of the students that have been assigned to them.

RECOMMENDATIONS

When the system is handled according to procedures described in this chapter, proctors can be an extremely effective resource for:

- Increasing the achievement of each student.
- Increasing each student's motivation and interest in the course.
- Extending the impact of the instructor's unique skills.
- Taking the pressure off other school resources (laboratories and libraries) by preventing these resources from having to be used simultaneously by large groups.

We would emphasize once again, however, that an instructor should have made some fairly basic decisions as to how he wants to teach the course before deciding on the proctor-managed system. There has been a great deal of successful experience in this area but there have been enough teachers, students, and proctors who have found themselves engaging in unproductive activities to warrant careful planning.

9

Use Of Peer-Proctor Systems

According to the information we've received, approximately 60% of those implementing an individualized system employ some form of student proctoring. Usually the proctor is a graduate student or an undergraduate selected from the population of those who have previously completed the course. Most professors prefer the undergraduate proctor because they have discovered that graduate students have a tendency to lecture.

However, a growing number of instructors are using students who are *presently* enrolled in the class as proctors. To the instructor, the most obvious advantage of these peer-proctors is that their use eliminates the requirement for obtaining outside personnel to help operate the system. In this chapter we will discuss some further advantages and disadvantages of two variations of peer-proctor systems.

THE ASSIGNED PEER-PROCTOR SYSTEM

In the assigned system, the proctors are usually chosen from among the better students taking the course. The proctor is assigned a group of his fellow students for whom he is responsible. This group (usually 10 to 15 students) remains constant throughout the semester.

An alternative approach is to have the proctor on duty at certain times during the week. The "duty" proctors do not have assigned groups, but serve anyone who shows up during their duty time.

The instructor usually recruits peer-proctors by asking for student volunteers from a selected population. This requires that the instructor identify his better students by personally grading the first fifteen or twenty Unit One tests. From this group he may then select those students he feels would make the best proctors, and ask them if they would like to volunteer. Most instructors report that recruiting is not a problem since students find the proctoring role a rewarding one. Some instructors add additional incentives for the peer-proctors by giving additional credit hours, bonus points toward a grade, or even pay.

THE ROTATING PEER-PROCTOR SYSTEM

A rotating system of proctoring was recently advocated by Dr. Gilmour Sherman of Georgetown University. As in the assigned proctor system, the first group of students through each unit is evaluated by the professor and these students are then asked if they would like to be proctors. The difference is that this process is repeated after *every* unit, so that a proctor's duties only last for one unit at a time.

For example, the first ten students who finished Unit One may be asked if they would like to be proctors for other students who have not yet completed that unit. Dr. Sherman has found that those that take the lead tend to keep it. So, many of these same students are the first to take the Unit Two test. Again, the instructor grades the first ten unit tests; and this "new" group, those that have passed the Unit Two test, are then asked to act as proctors for Unit Two. Dr. Sherman reports, "Even with the extra work of being a proctor they still get there first. So the ten proctor jobs pass back and forth between 15 to 20 people for the first half of the semester. Shortly after mid-term those students finish the course and disappear (although some enjoy the proctor role so much they come in even though they have finished the course.) As that first group of 20 finish up, then those who managed to stay close behind get their chance. (Note that even though they never made the "first team" they still get reinforced for keeping a relatively rapid pace.) And so it goes, through a third team and even a fourth near the end so that something like 60% of the students get a crack at it before the semester is over. Thus, all along the line there is a payoff for keeping up, even in second or third place, and as a dividend it does help with the procrastination problem.'' Dr. Sherman finds that any student who seriously wants to be a proctor usually can earn that right.

There are many side benefits to the peer-proctor system, although many students, when asked to act in the role of proctor, ask ''Gee, could I wait until tomorrow, I want to study the unit again so I will know it a little better.'' The phenomenon of a student learning better in order to teach others has been frequently noted. One peer-proctor, for example, had barely squeezed by at the minimum criterion level. She then graded a unit test for one of her peers whose comprehension of the unit was superior to hers. As a result she requested that she be allowed to restudy the unit and take a parallel form of the unit test.

As Sherman points out, peer-proctoring creates additional incentives for keeping ahead. Since the proctor is enrolled in the class and works for credit like everyone else, it is necessary that he complete a unit and be certified on it before he can act as a proctor for others on that unit. Under this contingency, peer-proctors in the assigned system have been known to complete an entire course in less than two weeks.

WHAT IS WRONG WITH PEER-PROCTORING?

Since, in peer-proctoring, you are working with relatively unsophisticated individuals, all the ''normal'' problems are magnified. Problems of reliability, responsibility and subject matter competency still exist, but one class of problems is somewhat lessened; that is, the tendency for the proctor to adopt an inflexible attitude and to lecture the student. Most proctors realize that since they are viewed as peers, fellow students are less likely to accept their decisions unquestioningly. As a result, they tend to defer more to the ''authority'' of the materials and are more likely to call on the instructor to resolve differences.

Many lively discussions occur in peer-proctored classrooms.

Instructors have reported that they frequently overhear the proctor attempting to muster support for the correct answer while the student is doing his best to support the answer he gave. Usually they arrive at a mutually satisfactory compromise. But this may have resulted only after several other students and proctors are drawn into the discussion. Of course, sometimes only by calling in the instructor can a point be settled. Most instructors are pleased with this state of affairs, since they have encouraged the students and proctor to exhaust every available resource and to consider the problem from several perspectives before consulting the instructor.

A MIXED SYSTEM

Several instructors have mitigated some of the problems inherent in the peer-proctor systems by using advanced students as supervisors. In such systems, students who have completed the course are given tutorial credit for acting both as proctors and proctor supervisors. These peer-proctors are often called "facilitators" to reduce the confusion in roles.

RECOMMENDATIONS

The peer-proctor system may be a reasonable alternative to using advanced students as proctors. The success of such programs depends in part on the attitude of both the instructor and the students. If there is a strong sense of responsibility on the part of the students, the program should succeed if the instructor is willing to give his trust.

The advantages of such systems lie in their economics and in the quality of the interactions. Those instructors who have used both the advanced student and peer systems report that peer-proctors will come to the instructor to seek guidance more frequently than advanced students and the proctor-student interactions appear to be more lively.

10

Individualization Within A Fixed Time Schedule

Many studies have shown the value of self-pacing in instructional settings. Group-paced systems are geared to the level of the low average learner, which means that classes usually progress at a pace too slow for most of the students but still too fast for a group of others. In spite of the resulting loss of motivation and performance, it is often difficult to break away from the group-paced systems because of the administrative convenience of such programs.

The advantage of self-pacing need not be abandoned entirely, however, just because of a necessity to observe scheduling requirements. It is possible to follow a fixed schedule, which defines certain dates when students must begin work on the same new objectives at the same time, but still allows each student to pace his own work in between those dates.

To employ the procedures used in developing an individualized fixed-schedule program, one must distinguish between *self-pacing* and *self-scheduling*. Self-pacing can be defined as:

> The ability of a student to *proceed through a learning activity at the rate he selects*, or letting a student determine when he will *conclude* a learning activity.

Self-scheduling is:

> *The ability of a student to initiate a learning activity at a time he selects*, or letting the student determine when he will *begin* a learning activity.

Thus, even in a fixed-pace system, i.e., one which determines when all students should *begin* certain activities, the student's program can contain a substantial degree of self-pacing if the student has some options in determining how long he will take to *conclude* each activity.

HOW FIXED-PACE SCHEDULES WORK

In one sense, almost every individualized course provides a fixed time schedule; that is, students are usually expected to complete their work by the end of the semester. This may be the only time the instructor (or the administration) insists that students be together. But this constraint imposes few restrictions on the degree of individualization that can be achieved. Almost every technique of individualized instruction still may be utilized.

In fact, the system can impose even more frequent fixed schedules and still provide for most of the forms of individualization. The most widely used form of fixed-schedule individualization employs a *weekly* schedule. For example, the instructor may insist that all students meet together at the same time on the same topic every Monday; but during the rest of the week, each student is allowed to go his own way, pursuing his learning goals at his own pace. If most of the learning activities accompanying such a system allow the student to complete them at his own rate, then an element of self-pacing is still being provided. There must be sufficient time between the initiation of each week's activities to ensure that the slowest student can master the concepts, but this is seldom a problem if a close check is kept on student progress, particularly during the first week or two.

Such a system was recently used for Introductory Physics by New York Institute of Technology (NYIT) in their research work at the U.S. Naval Academy. Figure 5 shows the general course flow and the progress of several typical students.

As shown in Figure 5, every student starts each new unit at the same time (Monday) and works on the same task; but from Tuesday through Thursday each student may pursue his learning goals in a fashion and at a pace he selects.

Figure 5

SAMPLE SEQUENCE OF EVENTS FOR ONE WEEK
(Starting a New Unit Each Monday)

	STUDENT NO. 1	STUDENT NO. 2	STUDENT NO. 3
MONDAY All students attend an overview lecture on Unit "X"	Attends lecture	Attends lecture	Attends lecture
TUESDAY Students select their own learning plan	Reads text	Views films	Attends group discussion
WEDNESDAY Students select their own learning plan	Views film	Reads text	Reads text
THURSDAY All students take a progress check test	Passes the test; then he rests until Monday	Is weak in Area "A"	Passes the test but wants to do enrichment work on Topic "B"
FRIDAY (SATURDAY)	"Rests"	Goes to a remedial lecture on Area "A" then takes a parallel form of the progress check test	Reads reprints and attends a special lecture on Topic "B"; then he rests until Monday

In order to provide for possible differences in learning styles and preferences, provision was also made to allow students to select their own paths from alternative learning experiences, all covering the same objectives. Since the Annapolis project was a research endeavor, there were sufficient funds available to construct many alternatives, an advantage not available in most schools. One finding of the study was that not all of these alternatives were equally valuable. For example, most students tended to concentrate on the programmed instruction texts and filmstrip, and bypass lectures and audio-tapes. The result was that many of the learning plans available were seldom used. Thus the project was valuable as a model — not of what should be done, but of what it is unnecessary to do.

MONDAY	TUESDAY	WEDNESDAY	THURSDAY	FRIDAY
Overview and Enrichment	Quiz A	Remedial Lecture	Quiz B	Make-up and Special Assistance
Students attend lectures, films, and demonstrations which are supplementary to text materials. Attendance is not required.	Students are given progress check tests; quizzes are graded by proctors. Results are posted by Tuesday evening. NOTE: Students who scored 90% or greater are excused for the rest of the week.	Students who did not pass Tuesday's quiz are given the opportunity to hear a lecture over the assigned material.	Second chance at progress check test. Parallel form of test is given and results are posted by Thursday evening. NOTE: Students who score less than 90% have two options: They may take the grade given or they may try a third form of the test on Friday.	Students who miss a quiz any time during the week can make it up on Friday. Also, those having special difficulties can consult with the teacher aides or the instructor on this day and then take the examination.

Figure 6

Another Sample Schedule

A system better suited to the resources found in most colleges is that advocated by Dr. Jack Michael, professor of psychology at Western Michigan University. Dr. Michael's system is also fixed-paced on a weekly basis but provides far more frequent opportunities for the student to check on his progress than does the NYIT system; and it requires far fewer resources. Dr. Michael's system generally follows the procedures shown in Figure 6.

Most people who adopt Dr. Michael's system employ a grade incentive to increase student motivation. Students are allowed to take up to three quizzes each week. The number of questions missed determines the number of grade points received as follows:

QUIZ A

Number of Questions Missed	Grade Points Awarded
0-2	10
3-7	1
8 or more	0

QUIZ B

Number of Questions Missed	Grade Points Awarded
0-2	9
3-6	1
7 or more	0

QUIZ C

Number of Questions Missed	Grade Points Awarded
0-2	7
3-4	5
5-6	3

There is an obvious incentive for the student who misses 3 or more questions on Test A to restudy the material and take Test B. A student who did fair on Test A (3-7) and very well on Test B (0-2) can still earn the maximum 10 points for the weekly quiz.

RECOMMENDATIONS

In this chapter we have discussed some of the methods by which individualized programs may be developed within fixed schedules. There are, however, some distinct advantages associated with more variable schedules that should not be ignored.

The most widely recognized advantage is found in the instructor and student attitudes toward variable scheduling. In most surveys, the feature of variable scheduling in individualized instruction is perceived by both professor and student as the most important single factor in the success of such programs. We suspect that students rate variable scheduling very high because it allows them to juggle their workloads. The instructor, however, sees a totally different advantage to variable scheduling. In the analysis of a recent survey conducted as a part of the research for this book, we found that instructors perceived the effects of variable scheduling as producing greater self-reliance on the part of each student. It is often stated that one of the primary purposes of a college education is to teach the students to become more self-reliant, that is, teach them how to use their environment to continue learning throughout life. Certainly variable self-scheduling allows for more practice in such behavior than does a fixed-pace schedule.

The second, and probably more legitimate reason for establishing a variable-paced schedule is to encourage students who may wish to proceed through the course faster than their peers. Many people who have used the variable-paced schedules report that a significant number of students are able to finish the course in far less than the allotted time. This is not possible in a fixed-schedule system, since in order to be "fair" such a system must accommodate the slowest students in the course. This means that students who are more proficient in scheduling their own time are being held back unnecessarily.

In general, we prefer a variable-paced system which implies both self-pacing and self-scheduling. If resources and administrative constraints are such that a fixed time schedule must be employed, the Michael system seems to be an excellent compromise.

11

Maintaining Student Progress In A Self-Paced System

One of the first questions that always arises when one is considering a self-paced system, or any other new instructional system, is that of motivation; how can one maintain student motivation without deadlines? Most people are surprised when they first learn that almost all instructors who have worked with a self-paced system cite *the ability to increase motivation as one of its chief advantages*.

Lack of motivation is one of the most powerful deterrents to effective learning, regardless of the educational system. And, the factors that tend to turn students off are the same everywhere. Within a self-paced system, however, the specific anti-motivating factors can be identified with much greater speed and precision. It is therefore possible to take specific "motivating" steps more frequently and with more direct effect.

To be sure, no system provides a certain cure for all motivational deficiencies. But only a brief comparison of the ways in which such deficiencies are recognized will show why they can be dealt with *more* effectively in a self-paced rather than in a group-paced system.

- In a group-paced system, such deficiencies manifest themselves in the form of poor or even failing grades, usually after it is too late to do anything about them even if remedial techniques are known. True, instructors can usually predict the problems accurately from classroom behavior, but they are not certain until after the student fails an exam.
- In a self-paced system, where every student must master each unit before proceeding to the next, the problem is seen immediately

in the form of stalling or delayed completion. Procrastination can be a major problem, but the very first time a student does not appear for a progress check at the expected time (about a week into the term) the delay is noted so that action can be taken. This gives the instructor an opportunity to provide help while it will do some good, rather than just award a punishing grade later on.

In this chapter we will describe the approaches that have been found most successful by instructors who have had experience with a self-paced system.

Some students can easily stick to schedules of their own devising. Others (even "good" students), enrolled in an independent study course for the first time, feel lost because of the lack of instructor-imposed deadlines. And since most of the students are enrolled in other classes that have regularly scheduled quizzes, term-paper deadlines, and so on, there is a strong tendency for the students to put off work that can wait (their self-paced class) in favor of work that must be done by a certain deadline.

On the other hand, if one of the major objectives of a college education is to instill in each student an ability to organize his environment for learning throughout life, then every effort should be made to teach students these self-management skills. This task is made much easier if the administrative structure of the school is set up in such a way that students can take as long as they need to complete a course since it is difficult to teach self-management to someone whose activities are managed by others.

Today, unfortunately, time constraints are present in most institutions. Compromises must be found, therefore, to accommodate the existing constraints. The problem is to ensure that a student has completed a significant portion of the course in the allotted time, or provide mechanisms for those who have not finished the course by the end of the semester to do so later.

KEEPING TRACK OF STUDENT PROGRESS

In most self-paced systems, performance is evaluated frequently. The results of the evaluation are transmitted to the student and translated into assignments according to the performance observed. One of the most effective (and fortunately one of the cheapest) ways to evaluate the rate of progress is to use a progress plotter which graphically displays the student's progress compared with the expected rate. Dr. David Born of the University of Utah maintains such a chart for each of his students. This chart (Figure 7) shows the number of units in the course and the dates on which the student completed each unit examination satisfactorily. Often more than one curve of possible student progress is shown. This allows a student to relate his own progress rate to more than one standard. Note that in this example, the student started slowly but soon exceeded the rate required to complete the course before the end of the term.

Anecdotal reports on the use of such charts indicate that whatever line is drawn, students tend to match it. Students report that they use the line in several ways. Some use it in place of the normal instructor-imposed deadlines and just pace themselves according to the line. Other students view it as a challenge. They try always to exceed the normal line. (This is why some professors like to add the second "rapid" line.)

In some programs the progress chart is used as an aid in getting the students to plan their own rates of progress. The student contracts for each subsequent test by indicating when he thinks he will be ready. The contract is usually worked out between the proctor or instructor and the student. Some professors even formalize the contract and ask the student to sign it.

POSITIVE INCENTIVES

One way to keep the students working on or ahead of schedule is to provide a payoff for them to do so. A very powerful incentive

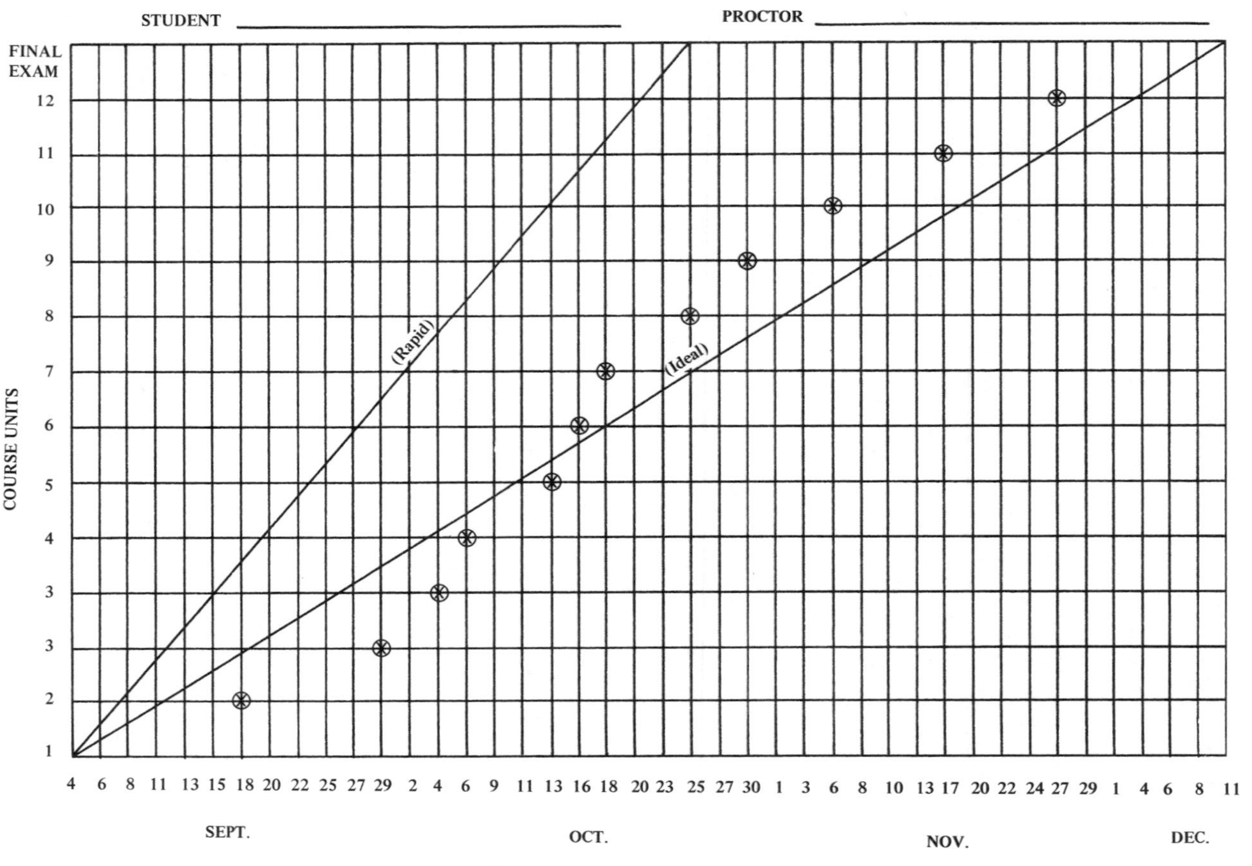

Figure 7. Cumulative Record of Mastery

for most students is the opportunity to complete the course early. For example, suppose the course consists of 12 units and a final exam, and students are required to master each unit before they can take the next, but they are allowed to progress at their own rate. There are two available options:

1. Students who have completed the twelve units can be excused from the course for the rest of the semester until the final exam; or, as an alternative:

2. An early final may be given anywhere from two to four weeks before the end of the semester for any student who has completed all 12 units.

Bonuses

Some professors take the position that the grade should, in part, reflect effort as well as achievement. Given this premise, it is reasonable to provide bonus points toward a higher grade for early completion. One method of providing bonuses is to give each student a standard schedule of unit tests and offer bonus points if tests are taken (and passed) early. The following example shows such a system:

SUGGESTED TEST SCHEDULES

UNIT NUMBER	DATE OF COMPLETION	BONUS POINTS FOR EARLY COMPLETION
Unit One	By February 2	6 points
Unit Two	By February 9	4 points
Unit Three	By February 16	2 points
Unit Four	By February 23	2 points

Note that in this example students who complete Units One and Two early receive more bonus points than for later units. It has been found that an early success experience is an important factor in self-management; habits acquired early in the term tend to be maintained.

Some bonus systems have even considered the possibility of using financial returns as incentives. It has been argued that since the student has finished early, he has consumed relatively less of the instructional resources; therefore he should be eligible for some form of reimbursement. For example, the student may be refunded part of his tuition. As an alternative, one institution has used additional tuition-free study as a form of reimbursement. Students who complete the course early may receive a one-credit-hour bonus in addition to the three credit-hours they have paid for.

Other Enriching Contingencies

Some systems provide rewarding activities contingent on satisfactory completion of a given unit of work. Procedures for such systems may appear as follows:

Complete unit ➧ Pass unit test ➧ Engage in rewarding activity.

When the student has completed a given unit of work and satisfactorily demonstrated his mastery, he is then allowed to engage in various kinds of enrichment activities associated with that unit. For example, a student who passes the unit test may be allowed to participate in a group discussion on topics related to that unit, or he may be eligible for laboratory activities, or attendance at a special lecture, or be allowed to do an interesting project for extra credit. In order for such a procedure to work, the student must have access to activities he finds rewarding. Unfortunately, what one student finds rewarding another may dislike. Many students, for example, like to engage in group discussions while others avoid them. To accommodate such widespread differences in student interest, some instructors have provided a "menu" of activities from which each student selects the ones he prefers. Some students, of course, prefer not to do *any* extra work. While one may question their motivation, an opportunity to take a break should not be ignored as a reward for achieving the course objectives on time.

THE DOOMSDAY CONTINGENCY

The simplest statement of the Doomsday Contingency is: "Turn in your assignment (or pass the test) by a certain date or you'll flunk." This, of course, is the contingency in effect in most classrooms today, and the widespread lack of motivation of which instructors so often complain is adequate testimony to its ineffectiveness. Most instructors do not consider that a student has given much evidence of motivation just because he has managed to get a passing grade by the end of term. But for students, grades are seldom as motivating as they (or their instructors or parents) believe. Problems of motivation start at the beginning of the term, whereas the "doom" (bad grade) will not come to pass until weeks or months later. This contingency can be used effectively, however, if it can be applied to stimulate productive habits frequently at the beginning of the term.

In a self-paced program, the Doomsday Contingency may state that the student should have completed the post tests for Units One and Two by the second week (Early Doomsday), or have met with the instructor to explain the reasons why he has not taken the examination. Any student who neither takes the test nor meets with the instructor will automatically be dropped. This contingency may have both positive and aversive properties; meeting with the instructor or proctor is somewhat aversive to some students. Instructors and proctors, however, are normally very supportive and provide encouragement for the student to catch up.

In most group-paced classes, the Doomsday Contingency is stated as: "The entire course must be completed by the last day of the semester (Late Doomsday) or else!" This implies that motivation and self-management skills are totally the responsibility of the student. Fortunately, most instructors want to share that responsibility whenever they can find a way to help, which is why most teachers find the motivational aspects of self-paced systems so rewarding.

ALTERNATIVES

There are many incentive potentials inherent in every interaction between instructor and student. Most are combinations of positive and aversive consequences. For example, in a proctor-managed system, proctors often prod students to do better. In the more productive encounters, this takes the form of saying, "You're a little bit behind. Why don't you make a special effort to catch up? I'll make a special effort to be here next Tuesday at 10 so you can take the next examination."

Sometimes professors use postcards to reach errant students. Some students will disappear and never report in until the last week to take all the unit tests unless a follow-up procedure is established. The probability of this happening is reduced if all students fill out several self-addressed postcards at the beginning of the semester. The instructors then may mail a postcard to any student who is among the missing, giving him an appointment for a conference.

There are also certain environmental conditions which may act to increase or decrease the probability of success for individual students. Obviously the ease of access to the proctors or instructors is an important factor. The greater the opportunity for personal interaction the better. Access to the place of study can be important as well; the more convenient the location, the more likely the student will be to take advantage of the services offered. One school, for example, has established a learning center in the basement of the men's dormitory.

RECOMMENDATIONS

Certainly not all students immediately become highly motivated in a self-paced system. Validation data collected on the use of individualized courses indicate that about 20% of the students start off preferring the externally-imposed discipline of stated deadlines, although that percentage declines with further experience in the system. This decline in anxiety occurs partly because *instructors have a greater opportunity to help* students who have not previously learned to manage their own time and effort successfully.

Very few schools make official administrative provision for self-paced classes. Frequently, however, instructors have an option of recording an "Incomplete" on the student's records at the end of the term, at least for a few weeks, which offers an approximation of a self-paced system. We recommend that instructors take greater advantage of this option. Even if the course is not fully individualized, with specially prepared materials, an element of self-pacing can be introduced with this approach.

At the beginning of the term, the students should be told that they may take an "Incomplete" at the end of the term and also be given a schedule of frequent performance checkpoints during the course. This will provide the instructor with a significant step toward a self-paced system and an increased ability to use incentives constructively to maintain student progress. Reasonable attention to student progress, *especially early in the term*, is usually enough to ensure that very few students fail to finish the course on time. However, if there are not enough resources to maintain this close follow-up, we suggest that the Early Doomsday contingency be followed.

12

Use Of Enrichment Activities

In discussions of responsiveness to individual students, one often hears the word "enrichment." It seems to be assumed that additional enriching activities are part of each student's needs and, in our survey of teachers' opinions, the opportunity to schedule such activities was often cited as one of the most important reasons for turning to individualized instruction.

The matter isn't quite that simple. In the first place, it is not always easy to know where course objectives stop and enrichment begins. In the second place, there often seems to be a legitimate doubt as to whose needs (the student's or the teacher's) are being served by scheduling enriching activities.

WHAT IS ENRICHMENT?

The term enrichment usually carries an implication that the student somehow receives a richer or more comprehensive learning experience. It is normally applied to certain learning activities which are thought to increase the student's understanding of concepts and/or provide means by which they may use their knowledge for a wider range of applications. In this sense, however, nearly all learning can be considered enrichment since almost every learning experience may lead to increased understanding. Therefore a definition of enrichment must also imply that it is "extra" or in some way different from other learning experiences. Sometimes the distinction is clear. When the core curriculum is well defined as that which *must* be acquired, while enrichment is in the "nice to know but not necessary" category, there is no doubt as to which is which. But in some cases, activities labeled "enrichment" are made a mandatory part of the course requirements, in which case the only difference may be that the enrichment activities are those that can be carried on without the textbook. Even lectures are sometimes stated to be for enrichment purposes.

Finally the question can also be confused when students are allowed to earn extra points by engaging in enrichment activities. Clearly this opportunity is of the greatest advantage to the fastest student, which may or may not be considered "fair"; but it certainly doesn't contribute much to the distinction between the learning objectives that must be achieved and those that are optional. An obvious question arises: If enrichment is something extra, why make it mandatory — and if it isn't extra, why bother to make the distinction at all?

This issue involves more than a play on words. If student performance is to be evaluated, one needs to know the standard against which the evaluation is being made. Those standards are presumably contained in the learning objectives students are expected to achieve and students do not always have a uniform view as to what those requirements are.

WHOSE NEEDS ARE SERVED?

We know of almost no one who would not agree that enrichment is a desirable thing to have in the curriculum. After all, who can argue that a richer learning experience is bad? In fact, just calling something an enriching activity is usually just about all that is needed to establish its desirability. In student opinion surveys most of the respondents say that increased enrichment would be one of the ways to effect the greatest improvement in the course. This has led many teachers to add enrichment activities to their programs. When the decision is made, however, the problem must be faced as to whether to make enrichment activities available for those students who wish to engage in them, to give students extra credit for those activities, or to make them mandatory. Dr. John Hess, of Eastern Mennonite College, implemented the first alternative. He reserved one day a week for enrichment activities which the students were free to attend on a voluntary basis. These sessions consisted of films, demonstrations, guest lecturers, and so on. Within three weeks the attendance dropped to only 10% of the students enrolled in the course and remained at this level throughout the semester. It appeared that even though students suggest that such activities should be made available (and Dr. Hess's students agreed with this) they do not attend them voluntarily. Dr. Hess then decided to grant extra credit for participation in these activities. He assigned a point value to each type of enriching activity available, the total points being averaged in with the student's test grades. The activities were still optional but, of course, unwillingness to participate limited the grade that could be achieved. The result was that participation jumped from 10% to nearly 100% of the students in the class.

When the extra work is mandatory, one can only say that the students' needs are served by providing enriching activities if one would also say that the students' needs are served by raising the requirement for course completion. If that is the case, it doesn't make a great deal of difference whether the work is called enrichment or core curriculum, but it probably defines enrichment in a different way than the students had in mind when they suggested that they would like to have more of it.

Another instance in which it is possible to question whose interests are served is in group-paced systems where enrichment is used to absorb the extra energies of students who are having an easy time of it with the regular curriculum. Often activities called enrichment are employed as a part of the custodial function of the school to keep students busy and out of trouble by giving them something that is (hopefully) interesting to do. Again, one must face the question of what is or should be required of the student.

ENRICHMENT IN AN INDIVIDUALIZED SYSTEM

As is true of any other learning activity, enrichment may affect either the scope or depth of a student's knowledge of the subject matter under study. Sometimes individualized programs are built around such precise behavioral objectives that they appear to be skimpy in their coverage. In these cases the instructor may feel that other activities should be scheduled as part of the course requirements to increase the scope and depth of the learning experience. Scope would be increased, for example, when a study of the techniques of psychoanalysis is followed with readings in the life of Freud. On the other hand, depth may be achieved when the same study is followed by the addition of material on the nature of schizophrenia.

In some cases, making enrichment activities mandatory can provide an incentive for the student to maintain continuous progress through the course. Professor Jerald Combs of California State University, San Francisco, used this technique in his individualized course in American History. Dr. Combs schedules a series of seven special topic sessions throughout the semester. These sessions may involve lectures, discussions, seminars, films, and so on, with most of the activities running from one to two weeks. The students may enter these special sessions, at least four of which are required for a passing grade, only after they have successfully reached predetermined points in their individual study materials.

If a teacher wishes to give credit for an enrichment activity, some measure of student participation must be used. These measures can range from a signed attendance sheet at an enrichment lecture to a progress check given after each enrichment activity. If the latter strategy is used, enrichment activities can follow the same structure as the core activities. Students sometimes contract to reach a certain performance level on enrichment activities, just as they do with core tasks and if they fail to meet the required standard they may be given remedial assignments.

RECOMMENDATIONS

The distinction between core curriculum and enrichment seems to us to have little practical value. If these activities are truly extra (optional), experience indicates that they are unlikely to receive much attention from the students. When students have time they tend to prefer to use it in other ways,either in activities they enjoy or in meeting the pressures of deadlines in other courses.

If the enrichment activities are not optional they simply become a part of the course objective, in which case the distinction seems to us superfluous. In fact, we suggest that it may be better to treat them as a part of the core curriculum and develop specific objectives for these activities as well. If the distinction between enrichment and core curriculum really only reflects the difference between those activities that are focused on learning objectives and those that are not, the student's interest is probably served to better advantage by abandoning the distinction altogether. We feel that the students' needs are best served in learning activities in which they know the objectives they are expected to achieve. We do not suggest that activities labeled *enrichment* are never worthwhile. The trouble arises when they are scheduled because they are desirable *activities*, which too often seems to exempt the instructor from having to specify the learning objective they are meant to serve.

13

Establishing An Individualized Learning Center

To most people, the term "Learning Center" conjures up an image of stacks of filmstrips, videotapes, and motion picture reels. Since the costs of such resources are usually beyond what might be allocated to any single college course, most professors do not even consider the possibility of developing their own learning center. But display media are *not* the key ingredients of a learning center. In fact, in some centers, such devices often gather dust because it is found, after the investment is made, that they contribute little to learning. A learning center should be concerned with learning, not the display of information. Many people are now beginning to recognize that a learning center need not be expensive; nor need it tie up considerable resources of the institution. Any professor who wishes to establish an individualized learning center, but has been restricted by the assumed need for expensive facilities, can do so. It is necessary to start with the basic premise that:

> *Learning can take place anywhere. Therefore, a learning center is merely an environment that makes the learning process as easy, convenient, and attractive as possible.*

This is not meant to imply that providing a space where students can watch videotapes or work with computers is bad but, rather, that there are other options which are often more important and which can be provided cheaply and easily. For example, a learning center can provide for more intense student activities such as laboratories, group discussions, individualized tutoring, etc. A learning center can also be a place where the student can get feedback as to his progress and receive assignments based on the diagnosis of his performance and needs.

Regardless of the subject matter or instructional approach, there are three things that must happen before learning takes place:

1. *A source of information must be available.* This means some kind of display or presentation device; a function which can be provided by a lecture, a textbook, a videotape machine, or a combination of such devices.

2. *The student must respond to the information presented.* The effectiveness of a learning experience depends to a large extent on the nature and intensity of the individual student's participation in that experience.

3. *Provision must be made for frequent and well-informed evaluations and diagnoses*, to ensure the best decisions in assigning new learning activities to each student.

This third function is by far the most important service a learning center can provide. As previously noted, instructional management is the real key to providing for greater individualization. To accomplish this function, the achievements, interests and abilities of each individual student must be assessed frequently.

A very effective learning center, therefore, may be nothing more expensive than an office or classroom where students can come to be evaluated on the concepts they have just studied (assessment). The form of the evaluation can be oral or written, subjective or objective. Whatever the form, the procedure must be designed so that the student can receive immediate feedback from the evaluation as to the adequacy of his or her response. The information gained from the evaluation is used to make decisions regarding appropriate assignments (decision). As a final step, the teacher or teacher aide must then inform the student as to the work that should be undertaken next (initiation).

Such a center requires no expensive equipment. All that is necessary is a room, a student, and an instructor or instructor aide. It is surprising, however, that many expensively equipped learning centers do not provide the fundamental requirement for evaluation and feedback; the assumption being that the sophisticated presentation devices will somehow teach.

Dr. Scott Wood of Drake University is presently in the process of opening a learning center. This center will be located in the basement of the men's dormitory and is planned to serve more than 600 introductory psychology students. Only two services are provided in this learning center; first, it is a place where students can work on independent study materials (e.g., read texts and complete workbooks). The second service involves all the activities associated with instructional management, i.e., frequent evaluation and the determination and initiation of individual assignments.

The center will be open from 9 to 5 each day, Monday through Friday, and from 7 to 9 on Tuesday and Thursday evenings. One proctor supervisor and from three to five proctors will always be on duty during this time. Dr. Wood will deliver a lecture approximately once every two weeks. In the meantime, students are free to work on their individualized materials at their own pace and in any setting they wish. They must come to the center only to take the unit examinations (evaluation) and receive assignments for new work, depending on the results of those examinations.

Students are required to pass each of the 12 units of the course with a score of 90% on their unit examination. Taking and failing the test does not count against them. They are only required to try again with another form of the test at some later date.

When the student is ready to take the test, he requests a copy from one of the proctors. The completed test is graded by a proctor, who also quizzes the student orally on some of the points in the unit. If the proctor is satisfied with both the student's written and oral performances, he will certify him for that unit. If, on the other hand, the student has not qualified at the 90% level, the proctor will point out areas of difficulty and indicate what kinds of remedial actions may be appropriate. The student is then free to come back at a later time to take a parallel form of the unit examination.

Dr. Wood operated a similar program the year before. He found that some students required extra help so he posted those times during the week when he was available in the learning center to help anyone having specific problems. Some students did their independent study work at the center because of the aid they received from Dr. Wood and/or the proctors. But as might be expected, most students did their studying outside of the center and only came in to take tests.

Often learning centers are developed through an evolutionary process. For example, Mrs. Lorraine Dieudonne of Foothill College in Los Altos Hills, California, has operated a learning center for some time. At first she used a conventional lecture hall, where she lectured on Mondays during her regularly scheduled class time. On Wednesdays and Fridays no lectures were held; instead, the room was open so that her students could take the unit tests.

Mrs. Dieudonne's program has undergone extensive changes over the last six quarters. By the third quarter she obtained a small room as a permanent learning center. Initially her program was very similar to that of Dr. Wood. Proctors were assigned duty hours and space was provided for students to sit and work quietly on their materials. By the fourth quarter, Mrs. Dieudonne had begun to add additional media and learning activities for the students. Tape decks were installed and cassette tape cartridges were made available for students who needed remedial lectures. As an aside, it is interesting to note that the equipment in this center gathers very little dust. Each piece was purchased *after* a continuing demand for it had been demonstrated.

This pattern of growth for a learning center is not unusual. Quite often centers are first established primarily for providing a space for independent study, or tutoring, then later for instructional management. Once the logistic and administrative problems associated with self-pacing are overcome, additional components, such as alternate display media, tape decks, slide-sound, single concept films or even computer terminals may be added. Achieving a fully functioning learning center requires that one must first break the lock-step instructional approach. Once this is done a learning center evolves as a natural process with increased sophistication being added gradually when it can be shown to facilitate the achievement of specific learning objectives.

The Multi-Discipline Center

Many schools now operate learning centers for multi-discipline use. The procedures described above apply to these programs as well. Most of the basic learning requirements are common to all disciplines.

It is possible to make a single-subject learning center multidisciplinary. The Mathematics Department at Drake University is considering sharing the same facilities with Dr. Wood's Psychology course for a Pre-Calculus course. It may even be possible to share proctors for some of the more straightforward evaluation and prescription tasks.

E. B. Loverin, Superintendent, Woodlake Union High School District (Woodlake, California), has set up such a center in which one instructor is on duty to handle evaluations and prescriptions for students pursuing a wide variety of subjects.

RECOMMENDATIONS

We believe every learning center should be started simply, using the most inexpensive means possible to achieve precise objectives, no matter how much money may be available for media. Funds for education are too tight for anyone to afford display devices that may never be used. The assigned classroom may be used as a learning center if nothing else is available. The major disadvantage of using an existing classroom, of course, is the need to set up the supporting materials and then remove them at the end of each hour. To solve this problem, several sections of the course may be scheduled back-to-back in the same room. Thus, if the registrar cooperates, an instructor may even create his own learning center simply by signing up for a given classroom space for three or more hours.

14

Alternative Grading Systems

Implementing an individualized learning system usually requires a special decision to select the grading system that will be employed. The system to which the instructor has been accustomed may not be compatible with his or her objectives in individualizing the course. Further, the change in the instructional approach may make it possible to use grading systems that were not previously available.

WHAT IS MEASURED BY GRADES?

In an individualized system, it is especially important to distinguish clearly between the types of performance the grades are supposed to measure.

Class grades are usually viewed as indicators of acquisition of knowledge and, often, of the student's effort as well. It is assumed that an A student has learned more, and perhaps worked harder, than a C student. The usual means of giving grades in college reflect these interpretations.

Final exam scores alone are measures of *acquisition* and grades are typically determined by a curve. To obtain a better sample of the knowledge acquired by the student, the final grade may reflect an accumulation or average of scores achieved on the four-week, eight-week, twelve-week, and final examinations. Grades may also reflect a degree of *effort* expended by the student. Some instructors give credit for the number of reports on books or articles, projects completed, laboratory work done, and so forth. In this case, we assume an A student was more motivated (did more work) than a C student.

The question of grading in individualized instruction may present complications. The instructional system itself requires a frequent evaluation of student responses in order to make new decisions as to a student's next learning task. This requirement may confound a standard grading system. For example, if a mastery contingency is imposed (i.e., a system in which a student can only progress by receiving an A for each step) it is difficult to justify awarding less than an A for the course. In such a system, the student has a far greater degree of control over his own grade. If a grade is based solely on the acquisition concept, then each student should receive an A upon completion of all the units. Many instructors, however, find administrative objections to such a program and therefore impose some other grading structure on the system.

THE CUMULATIVE POINT SYSTEM

The technique of basing the final grade on an accumulation, or average, of the test scores on the four, eight, and twelve week and final exams, is the most widely used example of a cumulative point system. As pointed out previously, the mastery contingency under which the student must earn an A on each unit in order to proceed to the next, is incompatible with cumulative grading systems. If the mastery contingency is removed, students are credited with whatever scores they achieve rather than being required to get an A on each unit in order to proceed to the next. Example One describes this familiar approach in order to provide a basis for comparison with other strategies that will be described later.

Example One

Assume a course is made up of 12 units. Each of the 12 unit tests has 20 multiple-choice items at 5 points an item — or 100 points total for each test. The course exam (final) has 100 items at 4 points per item, for a total of 400 points. The total possible point score on the test would be 1600 points, calculated as follows:

12 unit tests X 100 points	=	1200 points
1 course exam (final)	=	400 points
		1600 points

In this example, grades might be based on the percentage of 1600 points earned on the unit and course tests. The final grade for the course is determined as follows:

MASTERY	90%	(1440 points)	= A
	80%	(between 1280 and 1439 points)	= B
	70%	(between 1120 and 1279 points)	= C
	60%	(between 960 and 1119 points).	= D

The approach illustrated in the above example is satisfactory as long as every student has all the time needed to complete all the units. Most individualized systems attempt to allow every student as much time as needed to master each concept. Unfortunately, in many situations it is not possible to ignore time completely. A cumulative grading system may still be constructed to allow for time constraints. Example Two is such a system.

Example Two

Assume the same type of course as in Example One: i.e., 12 units, 12 unit post-tests, and a final examination. In this strategy, however, the final grade depends both on the test scores *and* on the number of units completed in the allotted time. A point rating, from 0 to 4, can be calculated as follows:

Complete 9 of the 12 units at the 90% level	1 point
Complete all 12 units at the 90% level	2 points
Score between 70 — 89% on the final examination	1 point
Score above 90% on the final examination	2 points

The total point rating would then determine the grade:

4 points equals an A
3 points equals a B
2 points equals a C
1 point equals a D

Thus, completing all 12 units (at a 90% level) and scoring 90% on the final would earn an A (2 + 2). Completing all units would earn a C without taking the final (2 + 0). Or completing only 9 units but scoring 90% on the final would earn a B (1 + 2).

Some professors emphasize time factors even more by giving A's only to those students who complete all 12 units at 90% four weeks before the course is over. Finishing on time would earn a B while taking more than a semester earns a C. There is preliminary evidence, however, indicating that students object to this sort of system.

COMBINING MASTERY AND EFFORT

In an individualized course, there is usually sufficient time for almost all students to master the objectives at the 90% level. Some feel that under these circumstances mastery of course content alone may be worth, at most, a C. This view holds that mastery of basic content is the minimum requirement; the final grade is determined by the *extra* work done.

In the third example, a combination of acquisition and effort (demonstrated by enrichment activities) is considered. In this system, the grade values of mastery tests are greatly reduced.

Example Three

The course grade is determined by the cumulative points earned in both the critical information area of the course and in enrichment activities. The final grade is determined in the following way:

A mid-course examination is added, worth a maximum of 75 points.

The final exam is worth a maximum of 150 points.

Each unit mastery test counts one point toward the final grade total.

An additional bonus point is given for each perfect score on a unit mastery test.

Additional enrichment activities, each worth a given number of points, give the students additional opportunities to improve their final grades. The following table illustrates a range of activities and appropriate point values.

	Approximate Number Available	Minimum Points	Maximum Points
Experiment	18	0	8
Reprint	20	2	10
Test Item	—	0	5
Lecture/Discussion	10	2	10
Film	10	2	10
Demonstration	8	2	10

In this example, there is a total of 302 points that can be earned during the course. Achievement of 250 points might qualify the student for an A with other grades distributed as follows:

A equals 225 to 250
B equals 210 to 225
C equals 190 to 209
D equals 175 to 189

SUMMARY OF OTHER PLANS

Recently, several researchers have done extensive experimentation to determine the *motivating effect* of alternative grading strategies (Hess, 1971). The following brief comments summarize the principal alternatives and observations as to their effects.

Strategy 1

Determine the grade for the course only on the basis of the percentage scored on the final test whether or not all units in the course have been mastered. This procedure permits a student to receive credit for partial mastery of a course by determination of percentage criteria for the comprehensive final appropriate for an A, B, or C. (A variation of this strategy would permit credit for partial mastery in terms of the ratio of mastered units to total possible units).

Observation: In this strategy there is no requirement for mastery of all units before taking the final. Thus, there is a tendency for students who are pressed for time to skip the mastery tests for each unit, concentrating on the last few units and achieving predictably lower gain scores.

Strategy 2

Base the course grade on the final exam (as in No. 1 above) but specify that all unit post-tests must be passed at the 90% level before the final can be taken.

Observation: Very few students who finished all the units under this system received less than an A. The necessity for the students to master each unit at a high level had a dramatic effect on their performance on the final examination.

Strategy 3

Allow a student who achieves a 95% criterion on all individual units to skip the final (based on the assumption that he probably would have met a 90% criterion on the final anyway).

Observation: This is a viable option only if occasional review units are built into the course materials and if security on the unit tests is adequate.

Strategy 4

Dispense with the final entirely and specify only that all units be mastered at some high percentage criterion.

Observation: While this strategy may be intuitively appealing to both instructor and students, elimination of the final deprives the instructor of valuable information.

a. The final is necessary if one wishes to produce comparative data on the overall effectiveness of a particular course relative to other versions of the course. (It is possible, however, to argue that this evaluative function could be adequately performed at the level of individual units.)

b. Final test data provide convincing documentation for those who believe that anything learned so easily and completely must be of lesser quantity or quality.

THE FUNCTION OF THE FINAL EXAMINATION

In courses requiring mastery of each unit, the final exams are composed only of questions related to concepts which have been previously mastered by the student. In this case, the final examination simply verifies a student's performance in the course. Some students, however, lack the self-confidence required to feel comfortable in a grading system based entirely upon performance on a comprehensive final examination. In classes made up largely of students who are not accustomed to success, it may be desirable to give a test after half the course units have been completed and to average these scores with those obtained in the comprehensive final. A mid-course test tied to a review unit would aid the student's integration of the first half of the course and would indicate concepts requiring further remedial study.

RECOMMENDATIONS

Our recommendation is to require at least 90% mastery on each unit test and 85% on the final; the student being allowed whatever time is required to complete all units and pass the final examination at these levels. If a student does not meet these percent requirements the first time, remedial exercises would be prescribed and the student would take an alternative form of the same test.

In what we would consider the ideal grading strategy, the term *credit* would then be entered in the student's permanent record with specific comments added in recognition of honors quality work or, if desired, of satisfactory completion of enriching activities. Often, however, grades are required by the college or by the students themselves. In this case, each student should receive an A whenever mastery, at the specified level, is achieved. An I would be recorded temporarily at the end of the term to any student who had not yet completed all units and taken the final.

Mastery is rapidly being accepted as the criterion for satisfactory performance in individualized instruction, and this grading system is the most compatible with that instructional objective.

15

Achieving Flexibility Within Administrative Constraints

Perhaps one of the most remarkable aspects of the innovative work that has been described in the earlier chapters is that it has been accomplished within, and often in spite of, constraints that tend to limit the ability of an individual teacher to make any significant change in instructional procedures.

Life would be much easier for teachers if they had only to contend with the problem of helping students achieve known learning objectives. There are, of course, a great many more functions that have to be performed.

Probably the heaviest additional burden imposed on the educational system results from the fact that schools are places in which students are required to spend a large portion of their waking hours. There are no other places where students can spend their time and acquire the training that society thinks they need. This fact imposes a custodial responsibility on the schools and teachers, requiring that they not only teach but also absorb, and direct productively, about 1,000 hours of energy per year for about 60 million students. In terms of time and resources spent in the educational system, this custodial function is often more significant than that of helping students achieve learning objectives.

Also, with the vast number of schools and a high degree of mobility in the population, there is no way the schools can avoid attending to such administrative problems as accreditation, licensing, certification and provision for transfer from one school to another. All these problems have become more difficult as the school systems grow larger and more complex. The increasing complexity has increased the needs of the schools for effective control over the activities of the students, and this control has tended to strengthen even more the requirements for the actual presence of the students on the school grounds.

Today the technology of education and the resulting changes in classroom management procedures described in earlier chapters has removed much of the need for the student's full-time presence in the classroom, or even on the school grounds. This fact is recognized in some outstanding programs, such as the "college without walls" in which residence requirements have been eliminated entirely. And the number of examples of programs demonstrating the reduced requirement of classroom attendance is growing rapidly; the British "Open University" and New York's "Empire State College" are recent examples of the trend.

Not all of the constraints are imposed by the schools themselves. State laws, accreditation regulations and local school board policies have been slow to change in recognition of the new opportunities. Most schools still permit enrollment only at the beginning of the term, insist that all students be given a grade at the end of each term, discourage the grade of "Incomplete," and fail students who do not attend class regularly. How can one operate an individualized class under these conditions?

These requirements, and the problems they create are common enough and yet individualized classes are thriving. This chapter presents some of the solutions instructors have found to the problems encountered in trying to introduce any significant change from the normal instructional procedures.

ATTENDANCE AND THE ADMINISTRATION

One of the chief difficulties a teacher faces when trying to get permission to individualize the class is the administrator's fear that this will result in a loss of income. The number of students in daily attendance is usually the basis of a formula used to compute the amount of money the school receives. It is often the case that, by law, a student can be counted in attendance only if he is physically in the presence of a certificated instructor and any reduction in the frequency of this contact can result in a loss of money to the school.

The California Legislature passed a law in 1971, regarding two year college students enrolled in specific types of classes, which modified the requirement for physical presence in class for the purpose of computing the average daily attendance. A student may now be enrolled in a class designated as a "coordinated instructional system" and still be counted in the average daily attendance figures, even though he may not be present in class at any particular time. This covers individualized classes, independent study programs, audio-tutorials, classes by television, and so on.

Even though some states do not make this exception, many colleges recognize that students enrolled in individualized classes are "in attendance" even though the entire class may be together no more than once a week. They recognize that the students are still required to meet with the instructor or proctor at other times and the fact that they are working independently is not taken to mean they are not working.

Obviously this willingness varies from college to college and from department to department. We know of many instructors who have hesitated to try individualized techniques in their classes, assuming that the attendance rule was inviolable, only to find out that when they asked for permission it was readily granted. It is always worthwhile to test the rule to see if it is as inflexible as it appears on paper.

Finally, in the event the administration insists that all students be present at all classes, it is still possible to move a long way toward individualization. Chapter 10 explains the procedure for individualizing within a fixed time schedule. It is entirely possible (the Psychology faculty at Western Michigan University considers that it is even preferable) to keep students moving at the same rate from week to week but permitting self-pacing of the activities within each week.

One faculty member at California State University, San Francisco, held to a strict attendance policy by the administration, assigned individualized materials only as homework and lectured entirely on supplementary and enrichment topics. With the confidence that the students were covering all the essential materials on their own she was able to capitalize on the enforced attendance to develop many topics which she had not been able to cover in her more traditional classes.

INCOMPLETE

Giving grades at the end of the term (or better, the possibility of not giving grades at all) creates another group of problems. Registrars tend to dislike the grade of "Incomplete" and computers are not usually programmed to store such a grade on a student's record for any extended length of time.

In theory, the students in an individualized course should receive their grade whenever they qualify — after 2 weeks, 12 weeks, or after a year if necessary. In practice, most colleges can record progress only in terms of the credit hour, i.e., the time spent successfully in class. A grade, an F if nothing else, must be given at the end of the specified time and an Incomplete often becomes an automatic Failure if the required work is not completed within a few weeks.

There are several ways instructors have found to recognize individual rates of progress and still give grades as required.

1. Many instructors make the final grade contingent upon the *number of units* successfully completed by the end of the term, eight units may be worth a C, eleven a B, all fourteen an A, for example, as described in Chapter 14: Alternative Grading Systems.

2. Some instructors make a special point of keeping their class on schedule, obviating the need for Incomplete. This can be done in a number of ways, as suggested in Chapter 11: Maintaining Student Progress in a Self-Paced System.

3. Some administrators allow a more flexible grading policy. A student receives his grade as soon as he has completed the work. He is excused from the class and may enroll in another (when possible) or simply have more time available for his other classes. A student who has not covered all the material by the end of the term is given no grade at all; or he is given a nonpunitive Incomplete. (Some schools use "IP"—In Progress—for this). He then enrolls for the same class the next term and continues where he left off.

4. A student may also, after receiving a grade of Incomplete, simply be expected to complete the rest of the material on his own. When the instructor certifies that he has successfully finished the course, he receives his grade and credit. While this works satisfactorily, it has several disadvantages compared to No. 3 above.

- Since the instructor concerned will normally have a full load of students in the new term, this student and others like him will represent an overload — an extra imposition on the instructor who may have to grade extra papers or even provide special assignments.
- Since the student must also register for a minimum number of hours to qualify as a full-time student, he too will have some overload as he attempts to finish off his "Incomplete" while maintaining progress in his other classes.
- The school will not receive the maximum state allotment since the student will not actually be registered in the class he is completing.

In practice, however, few students in individualized courses ever fail to complete the course on time.

CHEATING

Many teachers are concerned over the potential for cheating that exists in a course that relies heavily on objective tests for evaluation, and especially on tests that are not given to all students at the same time. Even in group-paced systems, several students working together can build up a complete test file in a short time; fraternities and sororities have always been full of such files.

In spite of the obvious potential for it, instructors in individualized classes rarely seem to feel that cheating is a problem. This is true even when the potential is compounded by the use of proctors and student aides, all of whom usually have access to tests and answer keys.

1. It is just about as easy to study as it is to cheat. There are (or should be) no trick questions, no guessing as to what is important. The objectives are laid out clearly in advance. The student knows what he must learn; and he usually has taken and passed a number of self-graded quizzes (progress checks) before attempting the unit test.

2. There is little or no penalty for failure on an examination. The student knows that if he does not come up to criterion level on his first test, he may restudy what he missed and then take an alternative form of the test. The test is no threat.

3. The evaluation often consists of something more than the written objective test. At the very least, most instructors or proctors will ask the student to explain any incorrect answers, or expand somewhat on correct answers. It is much more difficult to fake through an impromptu oral interview.

4. A few instructors have followed the simple expedient of putting each test item on a separate flash card. When the student requests a unit test, instead of receiving a prearranged test form, he is given (or asked to pick) a random selection of cards from the item pool.

5. Instructors who use proctors report that they make an effort

to substitute personally for each proctor from time to time. This allows the instructor, in addition to contacting more students individually, to check casually on the work of the proctors.

RECOMMENDATIONS

To achieve maximum benefit from individualized procedures, one should insist on regular class attendance only if the administration demands it, and cannot be persuaded to permit modification of attendance requirements. Ideally, students should be able to enroll in a class at any time and receive credit whenever they complete it successfully. Failing that, one can recommend to the Registrar the grade of IP (in progress) for students who require more than one term to complete the work. This IP should not automatically convert to an F after some period of time but should be carried on the student's record as long as work can reasonably be said to be in progress. These students should then register for the same class next term and take up work where they left off.

A note on the grade of F: It is our opinion that students should *never* be given a failing grade in any class. At worst they should receive no grade at all. They have invested their time, effort, and possibly their money, and they have nothing to show for it. That's punishment enough. The student should receive his grade and credit when, and only when, he completes his work successfully. This also eliminates the need for the grades of: Incomplete, Withdrawal, Withdrawal Failing, and so forth. It is a much more realistic and practical measure of a student's progress toward graduation. There is also a continuing incentive for the student to complete the work.

16

Some Of The Best Known Individualized Programs

It would take a book, or several books, to describe all the special programs that have been developed under the banner of *individualization*. Several more books would be required to catalog the improvements made by the tens of thousands of teachers who have felt an urgency to do *something* which would enable them to respond more frequently and accurately to each student's needs. All we have been able to do in this book is describe the types of things that characterize the largest part of those programs.

We are conscious that, by highlighting just a few programs, some readers will draw an implication that we ascribe to them a higher quality than those that are not mentioned. No such implication is intended. Every step toward increased responsiveness in education is a step in the right direction; "right" being defined as "consistent with a universally accepted goal."

Still, examples do help in illustrating the practical application of techniques and concepts so we will close with a brief description of some of the better known programs. The selection of programs, and the order in which they are presented, is intended to provide both an overview of ways in which individualized programs are used and a general feeling of the progress that has been made during the last decade.

INDIVIDUALLY PRESCRIBED INSTRUCTION (IPI)

The IPI System was begun in 1964 under the direction of Dr. Robert Glaser at the University of Pittsburgh. The original plan called for the development of an individualized curriculum so that teachers could prescribe different workbook assignments for each student. The areas originally concerned included reading, arithmetic and elementary science. The program was built around an achievement management approach. A redundancy strategy was used, that is, a sufficient number of similar exercises were provided so that if the students failed to master the objectives after the first several assignments, the teachers could assign more of the same until the students had grasped the concept. One of the most important pioneer efforts of IPI was its extensive use of teacher aides; usually para-professional volunteers from the community.

The Regional Educational Laboratory in Philadelphia, called Research for Better Schools (RBS), took over the curriculum development and dissemination project and further refined the materials and procedures. The program today provides a carefully engineered sequence of detailed behavioral objectives and criterion-referenced tests. The requirements for monitoring student behavior are still somewhat laborious in the IPI System but the constant monitoring of progress and continuing teacher diagnosis provides frequent feedback to learners.

THE PRIME SYSTEM

The acronym PRIME stands for the four essential components of a learning system; PRescription, Instruction, Motivation, and Evaluation. PRIME is the system originally developed by Donald Tosti and Lloyd Homme in their research laboratory in Albuquerque. The term "contingency management" was coined to describe these activities.

In the fall of 1964 the TMI Institute received a research grant from the Office of Education to investigate the use of programmed instruction materials with low-achieving adolescents. The original approach called for little more than setting the students up with programmed instruction booklets in a supervised study hall situation, and leaving them alone.

Within two days the project appeared to be a total failure; the students simply refused to go through the materials. One of the reasons these students were low achievers in the first place was a uniformly low level of motivation and completing a couple of thousand boring programmed instruction frames requires a good deal of motivation under the best of circumstances.

In trying modifications of the program to solve this problem, Tosti and Homme found that breaking the frame sequence into units of about 50 frames, testing and evaluating performance on those frames and providing a reinforcing (rewarding) activity for successful performance was all that was required to make the program a success.

The search for reinforcing activities that would appeal to a group of low-achieving, unmotivated adolescents demonstrated how it is possible to utilize very simple desires of the students and the necessity to try to see what is reinforcing to the *student*, rather than the teacher. One of the best ways to find out what activities the student found reinforcing was to ask them. Some preferences tended to change from day to day, while others had a more durable appeal. It was found, for example, that a student was very likely to finish a unit of work he did not enjoy if he was then permitted to spend a few minutes talking to an attractive typist. Another popular reinforcer was a chance to study the Russian language, on which their performance was impressive. This latter preference is not so surprising if one remembers that, in Albuquerque, the police are frequently conversant in both English and Spanish.

Shortly thereafter Tosti received a contract with the Job Corps to establish an experimental center. Capital Job Corps Center became the best example of a complete PRIME System in operation. The Center, established in the summer of 1966, implemented a comprehensive version of the PRIME model and became a training and experimental center for classroom procedures appropriate to implementing individualized instruction. One outgrowth of this effort was an Office of Education funded project to develop a series of prototype performance contract programs operating in New York City, Albuquerque, and Denver.

Today the PRIME system forms the basis of a variety of programs in addition to those used in performance contracts. Probably because of PRIME's close contact with Job Corps, the system has tended to be used most often in remedial or rehabilitative programs such as found in reformatories, prisons, mental hospitals, and programs for the retarded. The system has also been successfully implemented in private and public schools in programs ranging from pre-school to college level.

THE JOB CORPS

In the winter of 1964, Job Corps implemented the nation's first large-scale individualized program. The individualized Conservation Center Curriculum was eventually employed in over 100 centers throughout the country. The program covered reading and mathematics and was later extended into the areas of language, arts, and vocational and occupational training. Job Corps was the first to develop a comprehensive strategy for prescriptive management. Problems in curriculum placements were greatly magnified in Job Corps because the Corpsmen ranged from those who had never been to school to those who had some college work. The education program of each center had to accommodate this wide variety of educational experiences. Placement was done by a series of prescriptive tests, the outcome of which either led directly to a specific curriculum assignment or indicated requirements for more refined testing. To facilitate the prescriptive decisions, a series of flow charts were used, similar to the following:

Prescriptive Test Results
(Test Form P01)

Pre-test A	Pass	Pass	Pass	Fail	Fail	Fail	Fail	Fail
Pre-test B	Pass	Pass	Fail	Fail	Fail	Fail	Fail	Fail
Pre-test C	Pass	Fail	Fail	Fail	Fail	Fail	Fail	Fail
	↓	↓	↓	↓	↓	↓	↓	↓
	Take test P07	Enter math M5	Enter math MO	Take test P11	Enter math P04	Take test M2	Enter math M1	Enter math

The Job Corps also developed more sensitive strategies for achievement management than those imposed in individually prescribed instruction. Using the students and peer proctors as assessors, students were given progress checks after every exercise. Immediate feedback was provided and remedial prescriptions indicated by each progress check. Furthermore, a level advancement system was developed so that while a student was allowed to self-check his own work most of the time, there was still some form of teacher-managed decision imposed to ensure that the student was ready to pass from one level to another.

Failure to pass on the first attempt did not penalize the student or result in a poor grade. In fact, no grade was ever given. Students merely received remedial assignments which were designed to help them achieve their objectives on subsequent testing.

In later years a motivational management strategy called the Corpsmen Adviser System was added, in which student advancement was recognized by the use of a point system. Points could be earned from a variety of activities including educational achievement, work compensation, or engaging in special programs. Attaining a pre-set number of points earned the corpsmen promotions in rank which were accompanied by corresponding increases in salary. In fact, the Job Corps represents the largest "token economy" system ever developed.

NOVA SCHOOLS

The NOVA School complex in Fort Lauderdale, Florida, began as an educational park idea. But primarily because of the work of a few individuals, it soon became an individualized program. Today the curriculum covers the instructional program from kindergarten through college. The keystone of the NOVA System is the learning activity package, or LAP, which employs a prescriptive sequence similar to that used in IPI. In general, however, the NOVA System does not provide as detailed a procedure for instructional management as do the previously mentioned programs. Materials in the Learning Activity Packages are usually not as carefully controlled as are the instructional materials in the IPI or the PRIME Systems and, as a result, make more frequent use of conventional lecturing. The most pronounced aspect of the NOVA System is the emphasis on student participation and in the selection of each student's individual goals to fit his own personal aspirations.

NEW YORK INSTITUTE OF TECHNOLOGY

New York Institute of Technology has been working on Computer Managed Instruction (CMI) for more than eight years. The NYIT program, called AIMS, is defined as a computer-monitored system applying methods of systems analysis. It is so structured as to accommodate a self-paced mode of instruction.

The AIMS System provides information to the student, teacher, and course designer. Although the data can be used for several types of instructional management decisions, the student data are primarily used for achievement management. AIMS employs the computer to perform the acts of assessment and decision-making and leaves initiation to the student.

The instructor may query the system for individual student data, including historical data on any student's progress. He also may receive lists of students who have performed above or below the cut-off levels. Such data allows an instructor to schedule in-depth learning activities or may indicate to him a requirement for individual tutoring.

The course designer receives summaries of performance on individual test items and he may also receive historical data about student performance on specific learning segments to aid him in system modification.

NEW YORK STATE DEPARTMENT OF EDUCATION

A new system called Comprehensive Achievement Monitoring

(CAM) has been developed by W. P. Gorth and P. Schriever of the University of Massachusetts, and Robert O'Reilly of the New York State Education Department. It is a logical combination of prescriptive and achievement management. In this system, one year's work on a subject area such as elementary arithmetic is specified in terms of a series of objectives. Parallel test batteries are then prepared to measure student performance on these objectives. Students are given a complete battery at regular intervals throughout the year. Test results are assessed by a computer.

The reduced data on individual student achievement is then given to the teacher. The possible decisions available to the teachers are: to accelerate the student in the curriculum (prescriptive management), schedule remediation (achievement management) or provide activities which will give the student greater depth of knowledge (enrichment management). The CAM may also reveal a performance loss over time which would require the student to engage in additional review (maintenance management).

MENTREX

Mentrex was an operating Computer Managed Instruction System developed by J. Kirschenbaum of Fullerton Junior College. With this system, college instructors receive a catalog of test items in their subject area. The instructor prepares examinations by indicating the test item code number on a form and mailing it to a centralized computer service. One week later, Ditto masters of the test are received. Student answer sheets are sent to the center for batch processing. Within one week the student receives an analysis of his test. The printouts are similar to the NYIT System. The student is informed of his errors and given resources that he may use for remediation. He is also directed to essay questions that he should be able to answer when he has finally mastered the objectives.

The instructor receives a complete analysis of the test results including percentiles and a histogram.

PROJECT PLAN

Project PLAN was originally conceived by John Flannagan of American Institutes for Research. It was funded and is being marketed by Westinghouse Learning Corporation. Project PLAN does not supply learning material. Instead, Teacher Learning Units (TLU) specify learning objectives and pre-tests, and direct the student to the texts or other educational materials that are being used in the school. A unit test is given when a student feels he is ready. These tests cover content which would be expected to be mastered in two weeks of normal classroom instruction.

An interesting feature of one of the early versions of Project PLAN was its *level of passing* concept. These levels are:

1. *Pass* — which means the student may move on to the next unit.

2. *Student Certified* — which occurs when there are some errors but they are not of sufficient magnitude to indicate disruption in the program sequence. Students are on their own to certify when they feel they are ready to proceed.

3. *Teacher Certified* — which occurs when there is sufficient difficulty to indicate a need for student remediation. The decision to advance the student must be certified by the teacher.

4. *Machine Certified* — which requires that the student not only take appropriate remedial action, but he must also retake a parallel form of the unit examination before he is allowed to go on.

OAKLAND COMMUNITY COLLEGE

Oakland was the first college to attempt a completely individualized approach to instruction. Originally the program relied heavily on programmed instruction material prepared by Litton Industries and Educational Systems Development, Inc.

Recently Dr. Joseph Hill became President of Oakland Community College, bringing with him some of his research staff from Wayne University. Hill's research involves the development of a multidimensional profile of student characteristics (which supposedly identifies an individual's learning style). So far it has shown that there is a high degree of internal reliability in his profiles and they are used to assign to each student the presentation media best suited to his learning style.

The difficulty with this experiment is that to date there has been little or no data to validate these decisions with actual student achievement. It is not yet known whether correlation of media with individual learning styles results in greater achievement than having all students work with the same media. This is a contention of companies that produce sophisticated (and expensive) media, and remains to be proved.

THE KELLER SYSTEM

Over the last six years, Professor Fred Keller and his colleagues have developed and implemented a non-computer-managed form of individualized instruction at the college level. This system is also known as a proctor-managed or personalized system of instruction (PSI).

As in the PRIME System, the primary emphasis is on the motivation management aspects of instruction. The system provides for frequent evaluation of student performance by a combination of oral and written examinations. The criterion for advancement is usually near-perfect performance on both an oral and written examination. The data indicates that this motivation management strategy alone is extremely effective in producing greater learning.

Obviously some achievement management strategies must be used within the Keller System. In some programs, the proctors guide students to remedial activities; in other programs, the instructor holds remedial group sessions. But in most Keller-type programs, the responsibility for achievement management rests almost entirely on the student with very little formal guidance given.

CONCLUSION

We believe that the many programs typified by the examples described in this chapter and the instructional strategies described in this book give an impressive picture of serious innovation, *right in the nation's educational system*. Admittedly these types of approaches are not to be found everywhere in the system but a large start has been made and the use of these approaches is growing rapidly.

Criticism of the educational system will not stop, nor should it. As long as there is a need for further improvement, that need should continue to be highlighted. But such criticism should not blind us to what has been done. The most rapid progress toward the goal of responsiveness in education will be made by expanding the use of techniques already tested by the teachers themselves.

There is already enough innovation identifiable from this source alone to provide the long awaited revolution in education.

Module 1 Appendix A

What did you learn in school today?

Remember when you first heard the question? It was probably posed by your ancient (or so it seemed at the time) Aunt Emma (or was it Anna?) as she was delightedly twisting half of your cheek off your rosy face.

If you think about it, it is a pretty profound question.

The answer depends on many things. The information the instructor presented, the kind of learning activity provided, and most important, your level of interest and participation. The further you progress in your education, the more important the question becomes. The decision to participate and learn is yours to make. From now on:

IT'S UP TO YOU!

The idea of making your OWN DECISIONS may be a shock. Up till now others have made most of them, and they were usually right. Gradually though, the educational system in this country is leaving more decisions up to you! OUT OF THE BALCONY!
YOU'RE ON!!

DECISIONS, DECISIONS . . .

The process of educating people can be thought about in terms of the decisions that have to be made in order to teach a person something. Decisions like:

- WHO WILL BE TAUGHT
- WHAT WILL BE TAUGHT
- WHERE WILL THE TEACHING TAKE PLACE
- WHAT TIME YOU WILL START LEARNING AND WHAT TIME YOU WILL STOP LEARNING
- WHEN YOU HAVE LEARNED "ENOUGH."
- HOW MUCH TIME YOU WILL BE EXPOSED TO ONE TOPIC BEFORE YOU CAN REASONABLY BE EXPECTED TO HAVE "LEARNED" IT.

WHO IS MAKING ALL OF THESE DECISIONS??!!

Historically, the responsibility for deciding who learns what and when in American education has been given to the instructor. This works very well when:

1. All students are at the same level, and so, have to learn the same things, or
2. as in the past, there are relatively few students, allowing personal attention to be given to all.

Unfortunately, today's classes are too big and individual students differ too greatly to allow each instructor to do his best.

For example, suppose you (and your 30 classmates) are assigned a three hundred word paper. Suppose it takes your instructor an average of ten minutes to correct each paper . . .

Obviously, he or she will have to put in over five hours trying to tell you, in writing, just what it is that you did wrong. With the loads most teachers carry, there is not much time for real personal instruction in how to do it right.

IT'S A PROBLEM . . .

BUT

This situation is not as bad as it might appear.

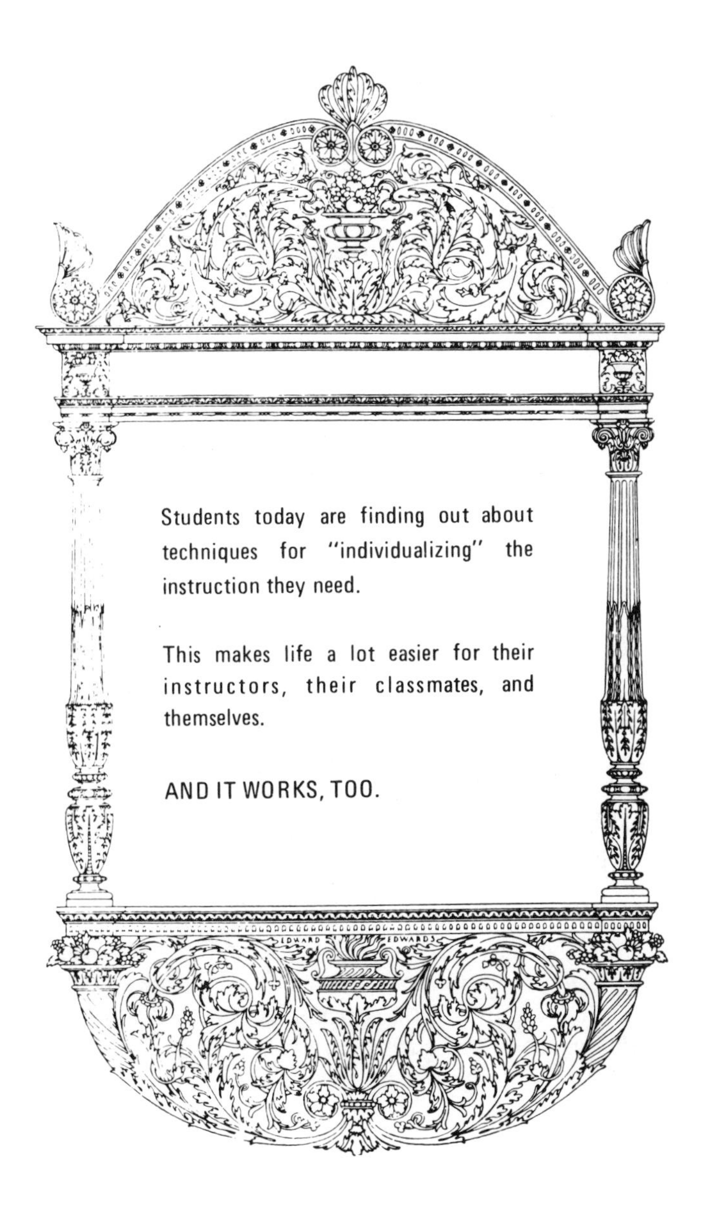

Students today are finding out about techniques for "individualizing" the instruction they need.

This makes life a lot easier for their instructors, their classmates, and themselves.

AND IT WORKS, TOO.

HOW IT WORKS

In most forms of individualized instruction you, the student, take on the responsibility for the work involved in learning. You need help, which the instructor or an aide provides, but you do the work.

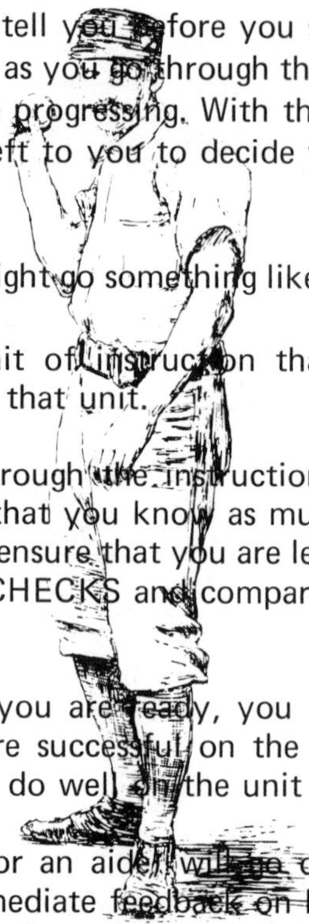

The materials themselves tell you before you start, what you are expected to accomplish, and as you go through them they will keep you aware as to how you are progressing. With that knowledge of your own progress, it can be left to you to decide when you are ready to take a test.

The sequence of events might go something like this:

1. You receive a unit of instruction that will tell you your OBJECTIVES for that unit.

2. You will work through the instructions on your own until you are satisfied that you know as much as you should. On the way, you will ensure that you are learning by giving yourself PROGRESS CHECKS and comparing your answers with the ones given.

3. When you think you are ready, you will be given a UNIT TEST. If you were successful on the progress checks, then you will probably do well on the unit test.

4. Your instructor (or an aide) will go over the test with you and give you immediate feedback on how well you did and where (if anywhere) you went wrong. Based on the instructor's evaluation, you proceed to a new unit or you delve more deeply into the current unit.

WHAT DOES IT ALL MEAN?

It means:

- You work at your own pace, not the pace of other students in the class.
- You have frequent opportunities to review your work with the instructor.
- You are able to find out for yourself what you have to learn.
- You learn only what you have to learn or want to learn.
- You learn much more quickly, and you retain much more of what you learn because you take a more active role in the learning process.
- You get instruction based on your needs, not the needs of "the typical student."
- Your learning is not bound to a schedule of lectures.

AND NOT ONLY THAT . . .

As you progress through the program you will find that you have developed greater abilities to manage your own time. As this happens it is usually possible for you to take on greater responsibility in deciding what should be studied and when. What this means is that you are becoming a much more independent learner. And this may mean more to you in the long run than the material you are learning.

O.K., now that we got the sales pitch out of the way, how does it WORK?

Individualized courses are divided into SEGMENTS, usually called "units," each one leading to demonstrated mastery of a particular learning task.

Contents

Unit 1	Laeyo aoio
Unit 2	Mnstr laeyo
Unit 3	mnstr laeyo
Unit 4	laeyo aoiou

In order to ensure that you are qualified to undertake each new task, you will have to demonstrate that you have learned each unit thoroughly before you go on to the next. At the end of each unit your learning is checked by the instructor or someone appointed by him.

What is Within a Unit?

The arrangement of material within a unit differs somewhat in the various courses, depending on the subject area. The basic format, however, is similar.

First of all, the unit is split up into smaller parts. These are usually called "modules" and are the building blocks of the unit. In some courses the small parts of a unit may be called "sections" or "lessons".

Straight Text

What a module is intended to teach determines its format. Often the learning part is in the form of straight text, as in most textbooks. This material, however, is carefully presented in a logical and easy-to-learn sequence. Frequently exercises are included as a part of the learning sequence; these may be anything from writing sentences to solving problems. When exercises are included in the learning sequence, they are very important because they increase the frequency of the student's active participation which, in turn, increases both learning rate and retention.

Programmed Text

The material to be learned may also be presented in frames; that is, the module may be programmed. If it is programmed, the course includes detailed instructions about how to do each frame.

Audio-Visual Material

In some subject areas, audio-visual presentations are a must. Film strips, cassette tapes, television, wall charts, transparencies and movies are just a few of the media that instructors may utilize. Some instructors even go so far as to conduct live lectures.

Instructional Material

So, every module, as you might have expected, has a part that teaches you something, or, at any rate, makes a start. This part, called the "instructional sequence," is followed by a decision-making device, usually called a progress check.

The progress check is a short quiz that you take, and grade, yourself. This lets you know if you have learned the material presented in the module; if you have, you go right on to the next module. If not, you will want to do some "remedial" work right there and then to make sure you are ready for the next task. You make your own decision, based on this progress check, about whether or not you go on immediately.

Remedial Loop

Suppose you did not know the answers to half the questions in the progress check. The answer key will tell you how to remedy the situation. From this key you may decide to restudy the module. You may only need to review specific frames in a programmed sequence, or you may turn to specific material designed to be used only when you have trouble with the basic presentation. The specific remedial material may be called an exercise or a sub-lesson.

If specific remedial material is included, a second progress check is also there. The second decision-making device is different from the first, but covers the same material. It is no harder, and may seem easier since you will have studied more in doing the extra work.

If you restudied the module or worked special exercises, you may take the first progress check again, at least the parts you missed, to make sure you have learned the material. Here again you make your own decision. If you are satisfied that you have learned it, you go on to the next module. If you are not sure, then you can either restudy the material on your own or ask your instructor for help or an explanation. In any event complete mastery of every module ensures mastery of the unit as a whole. The progress checks let you know where you stand.

Let's see now what a module does for you.

PRESENTS MATERIAL

TEXT

EXERCISES

1. ?

...

2. ?

...

EXAMPLES

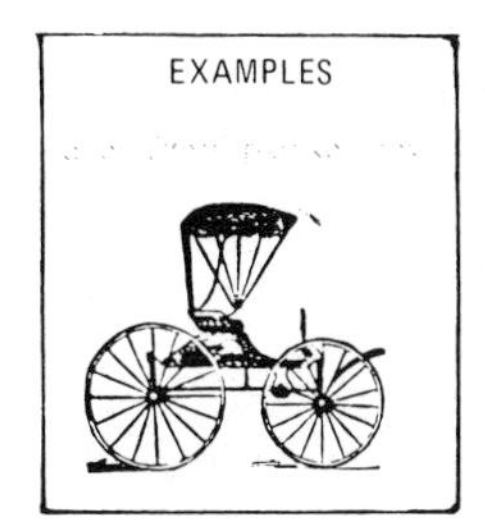

GIVES A DECISION-MAKING DEVICE

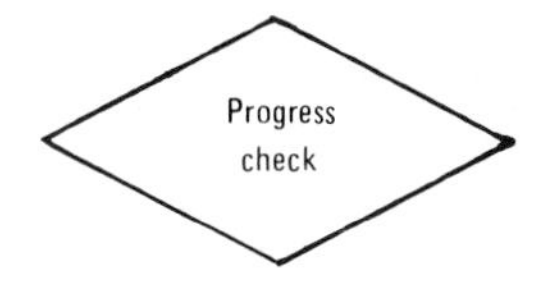

PROVIDES A REMEDIAL LOOP

Study Text Again	OR	Sub-lesson	OR	Exercises

HOW DOES THIS LOOK IN A CHART?

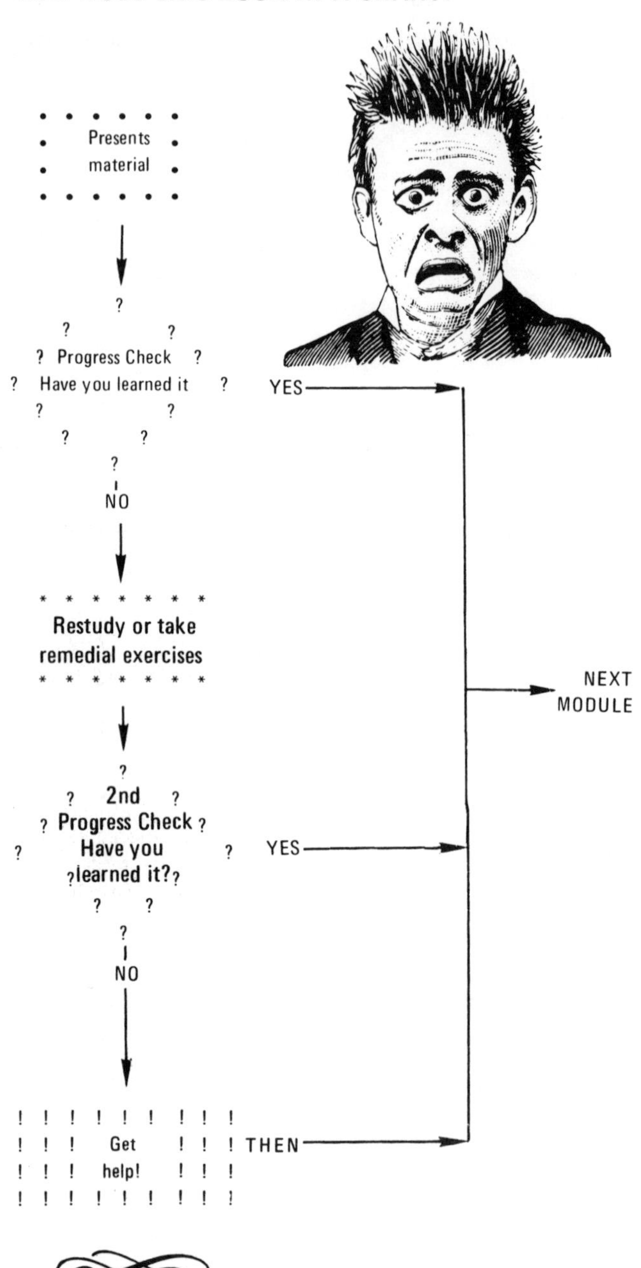

Specific modules, of course, may be a little different from the standard form. For example, many modules in a math course may include a short quiz at the beginning. This may be called a pre-test or a diagnostic check. Its purpose is to "diagnose" your abilities. If you pass this check, you can skip over the module and thus move more quickly through the unit. Units also frequently have optional pre-tests, so that you can really go through the course at your own speed, learning at your own rate.

Some modules may call for group discussion after a progress check, or some form of practical application of the concepts covered in one or more modules.

Basically, however, the structure of each module is:

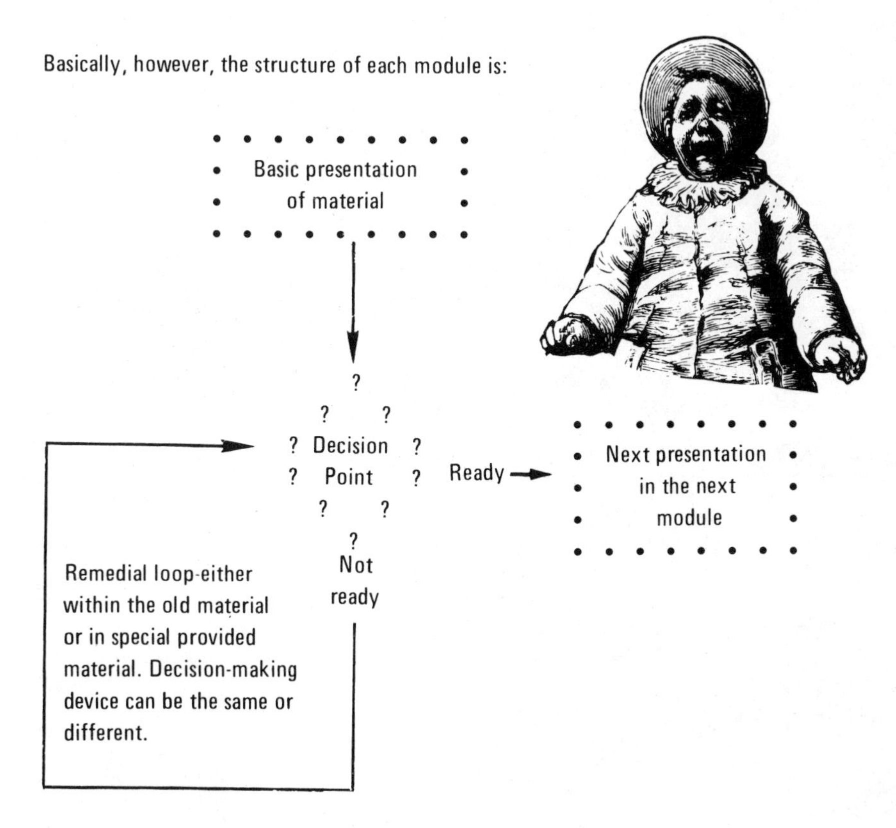

Unit Decision Points

The unit, then, is made up of several modules. In some Individualized Courses, the units also have a pre-test. The unit pre-test is usually optional. That means you can take it if you want to. The advantage of taking (and passing) a pre-test is that you may be allowed to skip all or part of the unit. On the pre-test you can show that you already know the material in a unit.

Units Always Have A Post-Test!

The unit test is THE BIG ONE, you must pass it before you can go on. The results of this test must be checked by your instructor, or someone designated by him (the aide may be called a facilitator, proctor, or teacher assistant).

You need not worry about these tests though. If you have studied the unit and been fair with yourself on the progress check tests, you should pass the unit test with ease.

O.K., suppose you don't pass it because you are sleepy, careless, or even forgetful. What then? Do you get dropped from the course, receive an F, have to wash blackboards for a month? No! You get a second chance. The instructor or an aide "prescribes" a restudy program; you will be told the specific areas you had trouble with so you can concentrate on them. Then when you are ready, you take the unit post-test again. This time you will get a different version of it, but the same material will be covered. It will probably seem easier, since you're better prepared, but actually it is of the same difficulty as the first. The fact that you passed the unit test is entered in the instructor's record book and you go on to the next unit. The test you did not pass is ignored. If you don't pass the second one, you restudy and then have a conference with your instructor. He will probably quiz you orally on the content and try to clear up your difficulties. Tests you don't pass don't count against you, but you can't go on until you have learned the material.

Let us look at a chart of how you progressed through the units:

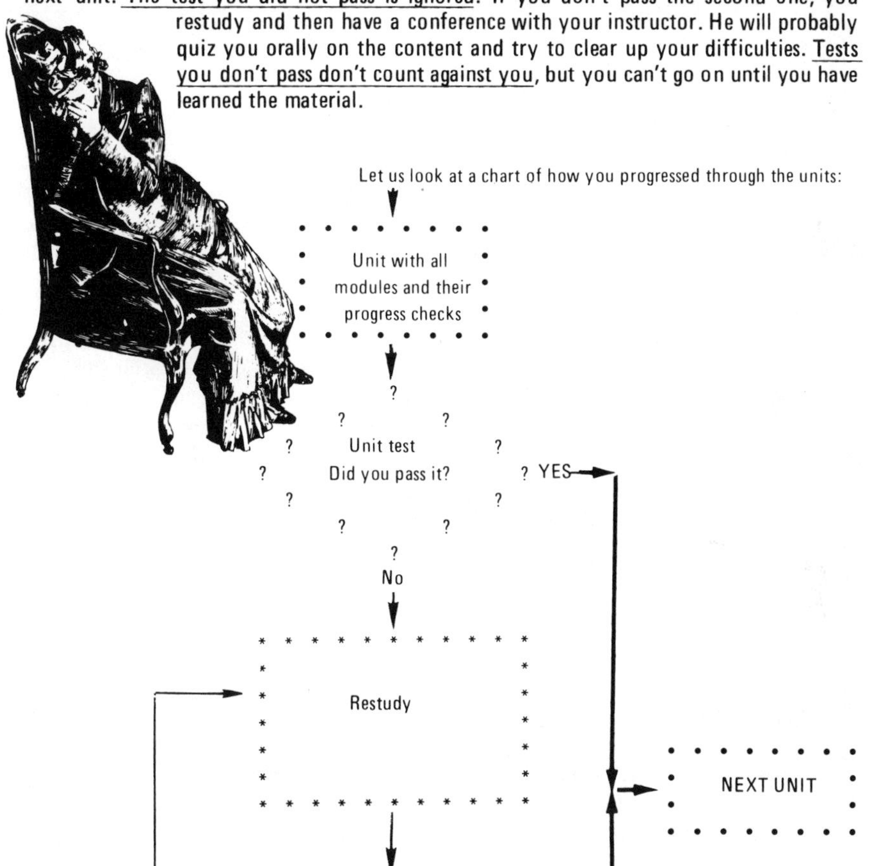

You can see that the basic form of modules and units is the same: presentation of material; decision point; and on to the next module or unit. The only difference is in who is involved in the decision. You make your decisions by yourself at the module level; you make them with your instructor at the unit level; at least the instructor is responsible for insuring that the decision is appropriate for you at that particular time. He may assign someone else to do it, like a teaching assistant or another student who is further along in the course. He may even ask you to make decisions on the unit level for students who are not as far along as you are.

So, at the end of each unit, the decision to go on is made jointly with some other well-informed person. At the module level, the student makes the decisions alone.

The Facilitator System

The instructor, as mentioned earlier, may grade your tests, discuss them with you, and make unit-level decisions with you. Or he may ask someone else, such as an instructor aide or student in the class, to function as a facilitator.

A facilitator makes the course easier and more convenient for both the other students and the instructor. He makes it possible for students to have more rewarding learning experiences in the individualized course. The students get help more quickly when they need it, and they can get the results of their unit tests almost immediately. By using facilitators, the instructor can let students who have already learned the material explain areas of uncertainty to other students and grade their unit tests. The instructor, of course, still is responsible for the quality of the decisions made about each student, so he will maintain contact with all students. But he may, for example, only need to grade every other unit test himself.

Any student may be asked to serve as a facilitator. However, if your instructor has decided to use this system he will explain it to you in more detail. The facilitators may lead group discussions if they are required in the course. They also can help the instructor keep records of the form of unit test taken by each student. In general, using the facilitator system gives all the students more opportunities for rewarding and informative interactions. This system frees the instructor for more responsible tasks than test-grading, while giving him more time for individual sessions with students who need his assistance. Whenever the facilitator and the student disagree, the problem is resolved by the instructor. Since the instructor remains in contact with the progress of all of the students, he can easily discover who functions most effectively as a facilitator.

Taking the unit test without being prepared hurts no one but the student; he wastes his time and is just sent back to study, and he must take another form of the test. Cheating on modules in an individualized course is cheating on yourself. You have nothing to gain, it just wastes time that could be spent learning.

IT'S UP TO YOU.

Progress Check 1

Select all correct answers for each question.

1. Which of the following is likely to be shortest?
   a. a module
   b. a course
   c. a unit
   d. a textbook
2. Suppose you are studying a module that has two progress checks and a set of remedial practice exercises. You finish with the presentation of material. Your next step then is to:
   a. go on to the next module.
   b. do the remedial practice exercises.
   c. take the first progress check.
   d. take the unit post-test.
3. Suppose you have finished all the modules in a unit. So you take the unit post-test. The instructor grades it for you, but you don't pass. What happens now?
   a. You get a zero and go on to the next unit.
   b. You restudy the unit, then take another form of the post-test.
   c. You get a zero, restudy the unit, and take the same post-test again.
   d. You have to repeat all the progress checks in the unit.
4. Match these terms with the definitions:
   1) unit post-test
   2) presentation
   3) module progress-check

   a. instructional material
   b. a test which allows you to skip over certain parts of the course
   c. a decision point where your decision is made jointly with someone else.
   d. a decision point where you make your decision alone.
5. A unit post-test may be graded by:
   a. the instructor.
   b. the student who took it.
   c. a facilitator.
   d. a student who has already passed the post-test for that unit.
6. A unit pre-test might allow you to:
   a. skip certain modules.
   b. skip a whole unit.
   c. skip the post-test for the next unit.
   d. omit the progress checks in studying the unit.
7. Suppose you are a facilitator. Your task may be to:
   a. help students pass the progress checks.
   b. grade tests and discuss them with the other students.
   c. be responsible for other students' learning.
   d. lead group discussions.

8. You are still a facilitator. You are grading a test and discussing it with the student. This is the second unit test he has taken, and he seems not to have learned all the material; but he insists that several of his answers are correct. What might you do now?
   a. Send him to restudy, then let him take the test again.
   b. Decide that he needs to talk to the instructor, and make the arrangements.
   c. Pass him and let him go on to the next unit since he seems very sure he is right.
   d. (none of the above)

Now, check your answers on Page 32. If you missed more than one, do the exercises beginning on the next page.

A Note About the Answers to the Exercises

The answers to the exercises are encoded and given at the bottom of the page so that you can easily check your answer after each question.

It is simple to check an encoded answer. Each question will be followed by a number in a grey box. For example: The first president of the United States was ______________. **2**

The number means that the correct answer will be found at the bottom of the page beside the box labeled 2, as below:

1 elephants and vegetables **2** George Washington **3** human rights **4** impressionistic painting

Exercises

(Select all correct answers for each question)

The chart below shows what you do in studying a module that does not have special remedial material included.

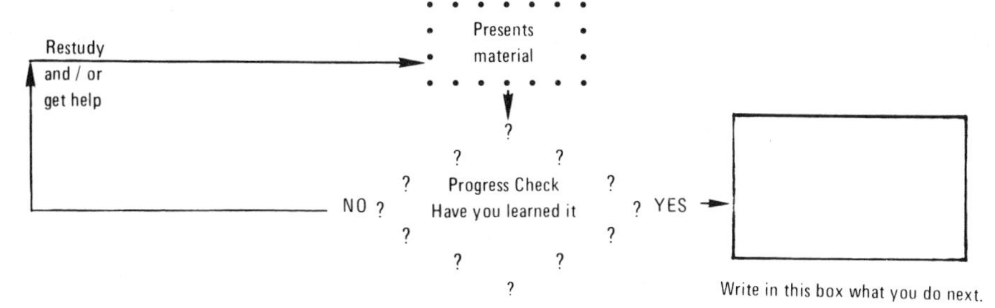

3

The chart on the right shows your path through a module that includes remedial exercises and a second decision-making device. Follow the instructions below.

a. Write in a few words what the first box represents.
b. Write the question that you decide the answer to in the diamond-shaped box.
c. Write what you do if you reach the box at the bottom of the chart. 1

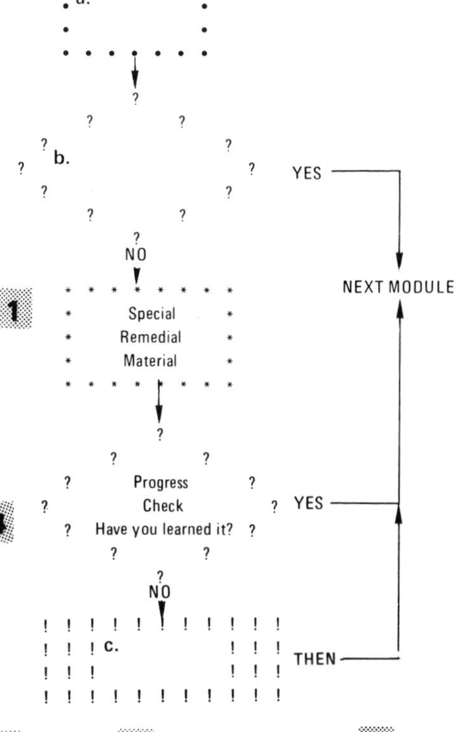

In this type of module who decides when you are ready to go on? 4

a. the instructor
b. the facilitator
c. yourself
d. the course itself

1
a. Material presentation or instruction, or similar words.
b. Progress Check. Have you learned it? Are you ready to go on, or similar.
c. Get Help! Or similar.

2 a

3 Go to next module

4 c

Which of the following is a decision-making device on the module level? **3**

a. the unit post-test
b. the presentation of material
c. the progress check
d. the next module

The chart below represents the basic structure of all modules. Write the correct letter from the chart before each of the following.

_____ The student studies the instructional part of the module. **4**
_____ The student goes on to the next module. **7**
_____ The student works practice exercises provided for remedial work. **1**
_____ The student takes the progress check. **2**
_____ The student makes his own decision. **8**
_____ The student restudies the module to remedy his learning. **5**

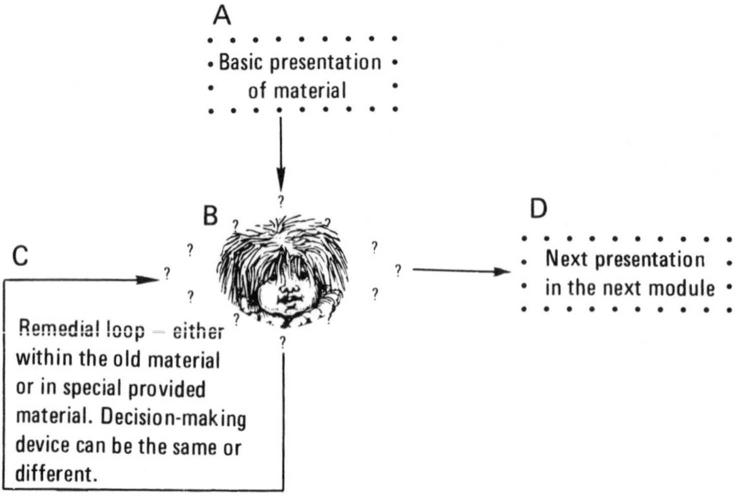

A
Basic presentation of material

B

C

Remedial loop — either within the old material or in special provided material. Decision-making device can be the same or different.

D
Next presentation in the next module

1 C. **2** B. **3** C. **4** A.

5 C. **6** A. **7** D. **8** B.

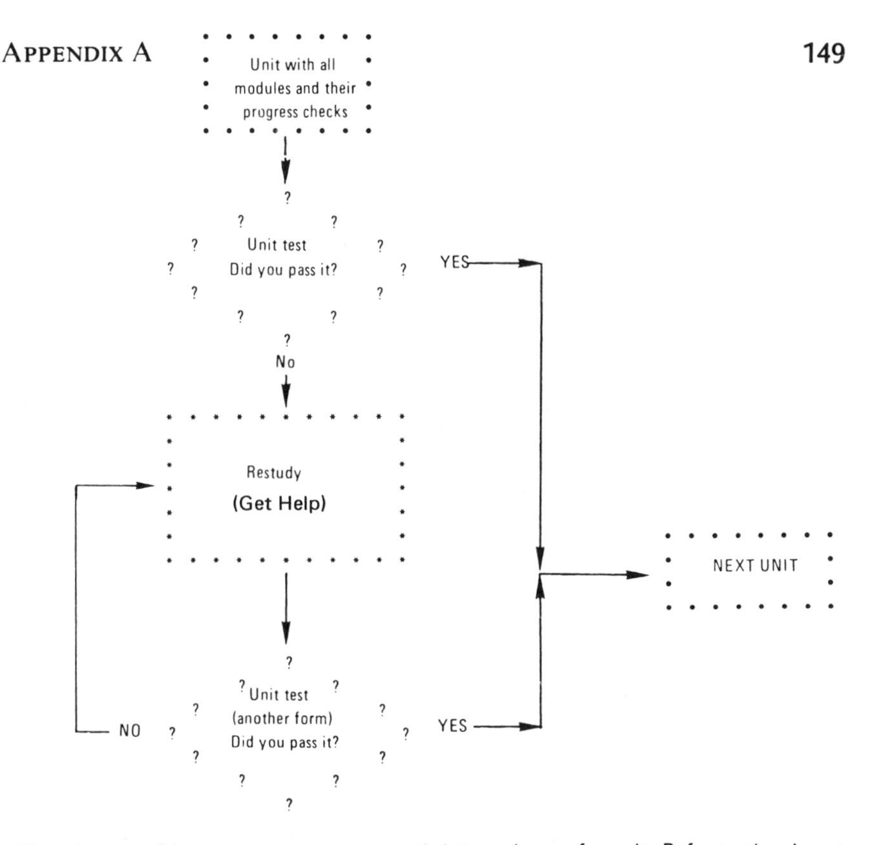

The chart on this page represents your path into and out of a unit. Refer to the chart to answer the following three questions:

The first decision point on this chart represents: **1**

a. presentation of material.
b. a unit test.
c. the remedial loop.
d. the next unit.

You are allowed to go on to the next unit: **3**

a. after you restudy the module.
b. as soon as you pass either unit test.
c. after you get help.
d. as soon as you pass all the progress checks within the unit.

The remedial loop for the path through the units includes: **2**

a. getting help.
b. a form of the unit test.
c. special material to study.
d. a pre-test.

1 b. **2** a, b **3** b, c **4** c,d

Suppose you take a pre-test for a unit represented by the chart on the preceding page. You get all the answers right; this affects your path through the unit: **2**

a. not at all.
b. by letting you skip only the first module.
c. by letting you take the post-test immediately.
d. by letting you go directly to the next unit.

Who may decide when you are ready to go on to the next unit? **3**

a. you
b. the instructor
c. the facilitator
d. the principal

A facilitator is someone who makes something easier. Which of the following might be a part of the role of a facilitator in an individualized course? **4**

a. The facilitator makes things easier for students by being able to spend time explaining things.
b. The facilitator makes things easier for the instructor by making decisions on the progress check level.
c. The facilitator grades tests he has passed and discusses them with students.
d. The facilitator is responsible for the learning of other students.

Suppose you are really in a hurry to get through a unit. You rush through the modules. You take the progress checks and miss lots of questions. You look at the answer keys and tell yourself, "Oh, I really knew that." The next day you take the unit test. What is the probable result? **1**

a. You get a zero and are allowed to go on to the next unit.
b. You don't pass. You must now go through the remedial loop before you can take the other form of the unit test.
c. You have cheated only yourself and are not allowed to go on yet.
d. The instructor gets angry and gives you an F.

1 b, c **2** d **3** b, c **4** a, c

Progress Check 2

Select all correct answers for each question.

1. You can make your decisions alone in an individualized course at which of the following points?
    a. a unit pre-test
    b. a unit post-test
    c. a module progress check
    d. (none of the above)

2. Which of the following statements might represent a decision made by a facilitator?
    a. Do the remedial exercises for this module, then take the second progress check.
    b. See the instructor because I am not sure what the problem is; you haven't passed the second form of the unit test.
    c. Go on to the next unit; you passed it.
    d. Lie back and take it easy.

3. You take a unit pre-test and pass all the questions about the first two modules but do very poorly on the questions about the other three modules. What might this mean as you study the unit?
    a. You skip the entire unit and go on to the next.
    b. You do not have to study the first two modules at all.
    c. You must study the last three modules, but needn't do the progress checks.
    d. You should study the last three modules in the usual way, taking the progress checks, and doing the remedial work if necessary.

4. The basic instructional material of a module is found in the:
    a. remedial loop.
    b. practice exercises.
    c. material presentation.
    d. unit pre-test.

5. Suppose you have taken the post-test for a particular unit twice and still haven't passed. What would you expect the facilitator to tell you?
    a. See the instructor about this.
    b. Come try the test again tomorrow.
    c. Study harder next time.
    d. Go on to the next unit.

6. Which of the following represent decision points?
   a. progress checks
   b. unit pre-tests
   c. unit post-tests
   d. programmed instruction
   e. material presentations

7. Suppose you are going through a module that has no special remedial section. You study the material, then take the progress check. But you get a few wrong. What do you do now?
   a. Go on to the next module.
   b. Do the practice exercises.
   c. Restudy the module, then try the progress check again.
   d. Restudy the module, then go right on to the next one.

8. Suppose you are sort of "cheating" on the progress checks in a unit by skipping remedial loops. What could happen?
   a. You might get an "F" for taking a test when unprepared.
   b. You might have to retake the unit test before you can go on to the next unit.
   c. The facilitator will know you were cheating and tell the instructor.
   d. You get through the course a lot easier.

Now, check your answers on Page 32. If you missed more than one and still do not understand it, ask your instructor for help.

IF YOU DID WELL, GO ON TO

MODULE 2

Self Management

Introduction

The system presented in this module is a result of recent research in self-management. It is a step-by-step system of self-recording and self-motivation which is called contracting. You use contracting to manage your studying by deciding what promises to make to yourself in order to achieve the results you want. A contract or agreement with yourself, a self-contract, will help you study both more effectively and less painfully. You can set up your own study system individualized by you and for you. To set up the system you need:

- GENERAL plans for all the classes you take.
- SPECIFIC day-to-day plans which will make it easy to accomplish each course objective in line with your own motivation at that time.
- SIMPLIFIED record-keeping forms, so you can see at a glance if you are "on target" to finish the class on time and avoid "crash-cram" end-of-term sessions.

This module is primarily for the student who is taking at least one individualized course. However, you can apply the methods you will learn here to planning your studies for any course.

Why Self-Management?

Every student has said at some time, "Why didn't I start this earlier"? Many students have also become painfully aware that a deadline for required studying in a course has come and gone. It is particularly important to solve this problem in an individualized course because, by solving it, you can earn the right to make more decisions as to your own study schedule—you can become an independent learner.

Good students say that they start each term with a plan. The plan specifies the studying necessary to meet the requirements of each course and indicates the sequence of studying needed. They report that they then "make a deal" with themselves to complete the studying on schedule. They do this by putting off certain rewarding activities until they complete the studying. A student may, for example, put off watching TV in the evening until he has accomplished a certain amount of studying.

Self-management of behavior has been shown to be of great value, but research indicates that it is even more effective when put into the form of a self-contract. A self-contract is a promise to yourself. You promise yourself to complete required studying on time and then to reward yourself with some desirable activity. The reward is something you have deliberately put off until after you complete the required studying task. Even good students often make the mistake of being "too tough" on themselves. They postpone important rewards for too long or until after too much studying. Not many students have the will-power to wait that long for a reward. The most effective methods discovered in study habits research include using short-term self-contracts with a reward for completing each one.

If you schedule your time early in the semester, you can self-contract the series of steps required to complete a course. This relatively painless approach to completing assignments also sets a rate at which you should complete units. It lets you show yourself your accomplishments.

To gain all the above advantages, a self-contract should include several things.

1. A list of the required tasks for each course.
2. A breakdown of each task into a series of small, specified steps.
3. A list of rewards which you will put off until you complete each specified step.
4. A written note to yourself giving deadlines for each step.

These points make up only the basic part of the self-contracting method. The following sections explain how to set up necessary parts of your own study contracting system.

Don't be too tough on yourself!

Specifying Study Activities

In most individualized courses, it is easy to decide what tasks and steps are to be completed. Completing each unit is a task. Each module is a step toward meeting the requirements of the task. For example, a simple listing of steps in a unit may look like this:

TASK LIST

Behavior Units	Deadline
1. Module 1	Sept. 17
2. Module 2	Sept. 19
3. Module 3	Sept. 23
4. Unit One Post-Test	Sept. 25

In courses that aren't individualized, specific tasks are not defined for you, so you must identify them for yourself. When you list tasks in such courses, be careful to state tasks in specific words that indicate progress toward a goal. A statement such as "get some work done on history project" is not too helpful. It doesn't state a beginning or ending point. A statement like "go to library and start on history project" isn't much better since it doesn't say what you will actually do. The task described may be only a reminder of a tentative plan of action. If this is true, why not actually write the plan? For example, the statement "go to library and make a list of references on trade union tactics" is a task with an identifiable completion. It specifies action that meets a goal and describes the actual behavior (writing) to be completed.

Specifying Rewarding Events (Rewards)

Doing something you really like (engaging in a rewarding event) just after you finish studying can be a powerful source of motivation. This is an important part of controlling your own studying. You should reward yourself after each study session. Be sure to select rewarding events (RE's) that are important to you. However, they should not be so valuable that you will take all or part of your RE before you finish your specified study tasks. The RE's you select should be short and easily accessible to you immediately after studying. Some examples are eating a snack, drinking a cola, listening to music, reading, and playing a guitar or other musical instrument. Some students keep a small fund of money available and take a specific amount after studying to spend on food or activity.

After you complete a certain amount of studying you should always take your RE in a specified amount based upon the amount of studying. Make a list of RE's. Decide how much study time will be worth each RE. For example, a 15-minute session of guitar playing may be very rewarding. It may motivate you to study an entire module. The self-contract, then, is a system of postponing rewards until a predetermined, specific amount of studying is completed.

Here is a list of some RE's specified by a hypothetical student.

RE LIST

Rewarding Event	Amount of Study Required
1. Work on motorcycle (30 min.)	2 Modules
2. Pool (30 min)	1 Module
3. Guitar playing (15 min)	1 Module
4. Eat fruit	2 Pages
5. Hike	1 Module
6. Phone calls	5 Pages
7.	
8.	
9.	
10.	

Money Available (Yes) No	$50.00 fund per term
Amount	Minutes of Study Required
$1.00 per evening break	2 hours

Putting the Contract Together

Now you have a listing of tasks with their deadlines and a list of RE's. You can combine these to form contracts. You can make up "Task Slips" for your contracts.

Contract Task Slips are used to remind yourself of daily contracts. Do not write complete tasks or steps on the task slips. Write only the behavior unit number from your task list. The contract may be for only a part of a module, for example. Write a summary of the task in terms of what you will do, and indicate the starting and stopping point. For example:

Date *Nov. 12* Behavior Unit No. *Math (2)*
Amount of Task *Finish Module 2 of Unit 1*
Amount of RE *Guitar - 30 minutes*
Date of Next Task *Nov 14* Contract Checker ______

The Contract Checker

The "Buddy-system" is well known as an aid to studying. When two students share and compare assignments, they give their personal strengths to a task and offset each other's weaknesses. A "Buddy-system" is also effective in individual studying. In this system the buddy may be called the contract checker. He shares the task of overseeing the completion of the other's contracts. In a typical system, two students help each other set up behavior units (tasks), RE units (rewards), and contracts for each other. You may find it helpful to have your contract checker give you your RE's. Perhaps you may even choose to share RE's after you both have completed a task.

Study Periods

You are probably able to specify a period or two each day during which you will study. Definite study periods are very useful in setting up a constant study rate. You should do some studying every day during these periods, even if only a few minutes. These study periods should be considered to be a commitment and a part of your self-contract.

Why Does it Work?

Many people have suggested reasons why self-contracts are so helpful in controlling studying. Most researchers agree, however, that self-contracting has three main benefits. First, the contract makes the student actually decide, in advance, the study pattern he will follow during the semester. This lets him see, early in the semester, the steps he needs to complete a course. This makes it clear to him how much time he must commit to the task. Without contracting, even good students may overlook or put off work until too late.

Second, the formal contract reminds him about coming tasks. He has summarized the term's tasks in his task list, breaking them down into behavior units. The contract's value as reminder of tasks is greater if it is kept in sight in the student's study area.

Third, putting off rewards gives that extra bit of push to get you started and through a study session. By delaying RE's until you have met your contract, you prove that you are in charge of your own behavior.

ARRANGE FOR AN EARLY SUCCESS

Old Aunt Emma also said, "Nothing succeeds like success." Passing the first unit test is the greatest feeling in the world. But many people often put it off; probably because most of us have some unpleasant memories about taking tests. In an individual course, however, the test should be a breeze. So, use every self-management trick you can think of to get yourself to take that first test. Announce loudly to your friends that you will take it on Tuesday, circle the date on your calendar, and promise yourself any rewards. Remember, IT'S UP TO YOU.

Progress Check

Select all correct answers for each question.

1. The first step in preparing for a contract is to:
   a. find a contract checker.
   b. locate a space to study in.
   c. make a list of tasks and steps.

2. The letters RE stand for a:
   a. Rewarding event.
   b. Review Environment.
   c. Remedial Examination.

3. Tom promised himself he would buy that record album he had always wanted when he completed four units of the English course. He had trouble starting the very first module and the contract failed. The failure probably happened because:
   a. it is always tough to get started on a new unit.
   b. buying the record album was not really a rewarding event.
   c. he is being too tough on himself by demanding four units before he obtains his reward.
   d. he didn't set up his contract in small enough steps.

4. Beside each task and step listed the student should write:
   a. how well he likes the task.
   b. the deadline for the task completion.
   c. a rating of how hard the task is.

5. From the list below, check all the items that would appear on the task slip on which you set up a contract:
   a. Date
   b. Instructor's Name
   c. Behavior Unit Number
   d. Your Name
   e. Amount of RE
   f. Percent of Course Completed
   g. Study Location
   h. Contract Checker
   i. Money Available
   j. Lecture Schedule

When you have completed this progress check, compare your work with the answer key on page 32. If you miss any items restudy those sections of the module shown next to the answer. Then try this progress check again.

Module 1 Answer Key

Progress Check 1

1. a (What is Within A Unit?)
2. c (Instructional Material)
3. b (Units Always Have A Post-Test!)
4. 1) c (Units Always Have A Post-Test!)
   2) a (Instructional Material)
   3) d (Instructional Material)
5. a,c,d (Units Always Have A Post-Test!)
6. a,b (Unit Decision Points)
7. b,d (The Facilitator System)
8. b (The Facilitator System)

Progress Check 2

1. c (Instructional Material)
2. b,c (The Facilitator System)
3. b.d (Units Always Have A Post-Test!)
4. c (Instructional Material)
5. a (Units Always Have A Post-Test!)
6. a,b,c (Instructional Material, Unit Decision Points, Units Always Have A Post-Test!)
7. c (Remedial Loop)
8. b (The Facilitator System)

1. c (Specifying Study Activities)
2. a (Specifying Rewarding Events)
3. c,d (Why Self-Management)
4. b (Specifying Study Activities)
5. a,c,e,h (Putting the Contract Together)

Now take your RE.

Appendix B
You Have To Play The Game
A Learner's Advice To Teachers

Note

As this book was being prepared (June 1972), we asked a 16 year old learner to write a short paper on the advice he would consider most useful in helping teachers to increase the learning that takes place in their classrooms. This is the paper he prepared.

His credentials to write on this subject include:

- Attendance at eight schools in three countries in ten years.
- Consistent first class honors in two of the most highly rated boys' schools in England and Canada.
- Total indifference to, and expulsion from, two other schools.
- Non-attendance at any school since November 1970.
- Independent study of a half dozen college-level courses in which he verified his achievement by taking the CLEP (College-Level Examination Program) achievement exams which are recognized for credit by about 1,000 colleges in the U.S. His lowest score placed him in the 85th percentile compared with students who had finished two years of college. His highest score ranked in the 96th percentile.

YOU HAVE TO PLAY THE GAME
A Learner's Advice to Teachers

I have become increasingly aware, during my career as a learner, of a difference of opinion that seems to be displayed in almost every school in the country, if not the world. Teachers appear to be convinced that there is something inherently enjoyable about learning, and students seem to be equally convinced that there isn't. This discrepancy is one main reason why students don't bother to learn anything at school (or as little as possible). Teachers believe that students should try to learn because it is so much fun and students believe they should be made glad in other ways that they learned something.

THE "SHEER JOY OF LEARNING"

I think the biggest obstacle to better education is the apparent assumption that good students study for the sheer joy of learning and that better education will come from producing more of the same. If one were to ask the average high school student whether he thought that this was very likely to motivate him to do anything, his honest answer would probably be an emphatic "No!" This contention is supported by my observation that not more than fifteen percent, and sometimes as little as two percent, of all of a student's time in class is spent actively trying to learn. The rest of the time is spent taking down homework assignments, transferring what is in the professor's notebook to the student's, examining other people in the class, gazing out the window (when he can get away with it), daydreaming (when he can't), or engaging in one of a great many pastimes designed to look as much like learning as possible, without actually committing the act itself.

Of course, someone is likely to say, "Everyone knows that people don't like school, but learning itself is lots of fun." This may even be true, if one is taking an out-of-school course in Shakespeare (and one happens to like Shakespeare). I have never heard of anyone who enjoyed memorizing a paragraph as an exercise, or trying to comprehend a difficult theorem in Trigonometry, or trying to recognize by sound the difference between a minor and a diminished seventh chord on a guitar. Although all of these things could be useful disciplines to someone, most people tend to learn them for that usefulness — not for the "sheer joy of learning."*

* Notice the words in this sentence, "most people." I do recognize that there are people who enjoy the act of learning all by itself. Some of these people make outstanding students. But they make up such a minor percentage of the total learning population that I don't mention them in this paper.

GAMES STUDENTS PLAY

In the last section, I tried to show the rarity of the sheer joy of learning. In this section I will present some of the methods used by students to get around tasks that this rarity makes unpleasant. One should remember that doing this (and still getting good grades) is an art, and a student's ability to do it deftly and smoothly is usually what makes an outstanding student.

In general, ruses and games for getting a good grade without learning anything fall into two categories:

1. Showing intense involvement in what the teacher is saying and the subject in general, and

2. telling the teacher how smart he is.

Here are examples of each.

Most students don't like to be called on to answer a question, and a sure way to be called on is to try not to be noticed. It shows interest and confidence in the subject always to have your hand up, so most successful students raise their hands on three-fourths of the questions, even if they don't know the answer. If a teacher gives a philosophical lecture about the sanctity of learning, or going to college, or underachieving, etc., a student can win favor by pretending that he really cares that he gets the message.

A good student always looks the teacher in the face while he is talking. Any indication that the student is listening to the teacher's lectures, i.e., a slight inclination of the head, suddenly sitting up straight, laughing at his jokes, letting out a gasp of surprise now and then, can motivate the teacher to change a fail to a pass, or a B to an A.

One game that is not widespread but that I used quite extensively was to take every opportunity to show a great difference in my relationship with the teacher when I was out of class from when I was in. This let the teacher know that, although I thought he was a grand guy, when we were in class he was a revered and respected all-wise monarch. I don't think this raised my grades much but I'm sure it put me solidly in his favor.

At one point in grade school, I was particularly bored and slightly confused by mathematics. One morning I arrived at school with my homework undone. I stormed into the classroom, appearing furious and frustrated, and announced to the teacher that the math textbook was useless, and I could not make head or tail of the subject matter the class was going through (not mentioning my homework assignment). Before the class started, he patiently explained the material to me, and during a period of about five minutes, I let myself be brought from complete confusion to an A student's understanding of the subject. The teacher must have thought himself a genius, and he neglected to notice that I had not completed my homework.

This method is used in simpler form by students who monopolize class time asking questions to which they already know the answer. A student only needs to study one-tenth of his reading assignment and ask a barrage of questions about that one-tenth, to flatter the teacher into a good grade.

One last deceptively simple ruse is that a good student tries never to let a negative emotion escape in class, unless it is the type that a teacher will think he ought to do something about. Frustration and maybe a small amount of hopelessness tend to produce this reaction.

OUTSMARTING THE STUDENTS

Successful students seem to regard school as a big game (more or less consciously) and are able to get good grades for an absolute minimum of effort and even less learning. I would say that this was only partly a function of the deficiencies in the present school system. I would also say that, if the students are playing a game, then the teachers should recognize it for what it is, and get in on it, too.

Making people do what you want them to is a large and important facet of Western society. A man who is clever at it is more likely to be successful in his pursuits than a man who is not. A boy who grows up with this viewpoint all his life, and practices it in school, will probably be the man who is clever at it. And that boy is more likely to have that viewpoint if it is encouraged and preferably shared by his teacher.

One should worry, however, whether this game is conducive to learning. Until now it has been used to get out of learning. It all depends on how you define the rules. Below are two sets of rules. The first is the set as now applied and the second are my proposed rules.

CURRENT

To get *good grades*, one must:

1. Smile in class
2. Appear to be listening
3. Keep your hand in the air
4. Ask lots of questions that you already can answer
5. Show respect for the teacher
6. Generally act in accordance with the rules

To get *extra favors*, one must:

1. Smile out of class.
2. Appear cute or of equal intelligence
3. Generally act in accordance with the rules

PROPOSED

To get *good grades plus*, one must:

1. Show complete understanding and mastery of the proper material

To get *extra favors*, one must:

1. Smile out of class.
2. Act in a fashion that will impress rather than just titillate the teacher.
3. Appear to be listening.
4. Generally act in accordance with the rules.

It seems obvious to me that the proposed set of rules will produce more learning than those currently in use. The problem, or so it seems, lies in letting the students know that the rules have been changed.

First, one has to decide exactly what a student gets for his effort. Extra favors means things like having coffee in the faculty lounge —a personal expression of gratitude on the part of the teacher. Good grades plus means that the student gets good grades for all the things he *should* be doing right now, but he also gets something else that means more to him. Every school has activities (subjects?) that students enjoy — and right now are given free. These activities could be made contingent upon getting a good grade. This means that the student can only go to his P.E. or music class when he has finished the math or English work he has been assigned for the day to a suitably high standard. The things students enjoy should not be given equally to everyone without consideration of their performance on assigned work.

SUMMARY

There is an old story about holding a carrot at the end of a stick and making a donkey walk. I don't know if it works. I *do* know that if the donkey likes carrots and he is given one after 200 paces he is more likely to take the next 200 paces. The same thing can be said of students.

Earlier I mentioned that I believe there are *some* students who simply have a pervasive desire to learn. But these are very few and far between. Most kids would rather have their carrot every 200 paces than the "sheer joy of learning."

Appendix C
Neglected Rewards in The Educational Process

Dr. Fred S Keller
Columbia University*

I am not at all certain that I should be here today. I have no inspirational message to impart, no over-arching principle with which to span the realms of art and science, and no skill whatever as a public entertainer. Worst of all, I have no faith in the lecture system as a device for conveying information, and am therefore acting against my own judgment. Or perhaps I'm here simply as an old educational reformer with a devotion to one idea that has been equalled only by such historical figures as Ignaz Semmelweis, Johnny Appleseed, and "Indian-lover" George Catlin.

Five years ago, I was beginning to move in the direction of retirement. My working days were getting shorter and my output smaller; I was reading less in the technical journals; I was avoiding committee memberships and administrative chores; and I was looking for a place where my Teacher's Annuity and my Social Security income would permit my wife and me to round out our years in all the comfort to which we were accustomed. Then, quite suddenly, I was asked to join with three younger colleagues (two Brazilians and an American)[1] in setting up a department of psychology at the New University of Brasilia, in Brazil's capital city. The Minister of Education offered *carta blanca* to the group; he promised all the space and money that we might require; and he encouraged us to adopt an experimental attitude with respect to the curriculum and the procedures of instruction.

* The author is presently at Western Michigan University, Kalamazoo, Michigan.

It was impossible to turn down this opportunity. Within a few months, my three colleagues were in this country buying books and equipment, visiting laboratories, libraries, machine shops, hospitals, and classrooms, asking questions of everyone concerning curriculum content, course sequences, desirable textbooks, and methods of teaching. Finally, as the time drew near for the first classes to begin in the new University, we took up the specific issue of the introductory course — what it should contain and how it should be taught.

Out of our discussions came a new method of teaching — new, at least, to us. It was tried out first, within a formal academic setting, at Brasilia, in 1964. Soon after this, in the Spring of '65, it was used at Arizona State University.[2] Since then, it has been continued, with minor modifications, at Arizona State, and has been introduced at a few other institutions in an exploratory fashion.

Because the method shows some promise in other areas and at other levels than that of introductory psychology; because it is probably typical of many attacks upon the teaching problem that will plague you in the coming years; and, because Dean Lichtenstein has opened the door for me to do so, I am going to describe this method to you now. In addition, I shall discuss some of the reactions to it, by students and others; I shall comment briefly upon its relation to earlier teaching practices and to modern learning theory; and I shall end by mentioning one or two of its defects.

I'll begin by asking you to imagine, if you can, that you are once again a college freshman. You have just arrived, along with nearly a hundred other students, men and women, at the first meeting of a one-term course in elementary psychology, with laboratory. This is a four-credit course, with seventy-five-minute meetings scheduled for Tuesdays and Thursdays, and with ten laboratory sessions to be carried out during designated hours of the coming term.

At this first class meeting, you are given a brief description of the origins, the aims, and the general procedure of the course. You are introduced to the members of the staff, and, finally, you are given a mimeographed hand-out form which I would like to quote at this time. (In Brasilia, this ritual included a round of coffee for all the students.)

"This is a course through which you may move, from start to finish, at your own pace. You will not be held back by other students or forced to go ahead until you are ready. At best, you may meet all the course requirements in less than one semester; at worst, you may not complete the job within that time. How fast you go is up to you.

"The work of this course will be divided into thirty units of content, which correspond roughly to a series of homework assignments and laboratory exercises. These units will come in a definite numerical order, and *you must show your mastery of each unit, by passing a readiness test or carrying out an experiment, before moving on to the next . . .*

"The lectures and demonstrations in this course will have a different relation to the rest of your work than is usually the rule. They will be provided only when you have demonstrated your readiness to appreciate them; no examination will be based upon them; and you need not attend them if you do not wish . . .

"The teaching staff of your course will include proctors, assistants, and an instructor. A *proctor* is an undergraduate who has been chosen for his mastery of the course content and orientation, for his maturity of judgment, for his understanding of the special problems that confront you as a beginner, for his willingness to assist. He will provide you with all your study materials except your textbooks. He will pass upon your readiness tests as satisfactory or unsatisfactory. His judgment will ordinarily be law, but if he is ever in serious doubt, he can appeal to the classroom assistant for a ruling, or even to the instructor. *Failure to pass a test on the first try, the second, the third, or even later, will not be held against you. It is better that you get too much testing than not enough*, if your final success is to be assured . .

"There will also be a graduate *classroom assistant*, upon whom your proctor will depend for course assignments, study questions, special reading, and so on, and who will collect and keep up to date all progress records for course members. The classroom assistant will confer with the instructor daily, aid the proctors on occasion, and act in a variety of ways to further the smooth operation of the course machinery.

"All students in the course are expected to take a final examination, in which the entire term's work will be represented. With certain exceptions, this examination will come at the same time for all students, at the end of the term. The examination will consist of questions which, in large part, you have already answered in your readiness tests. Twenty-five percent of your course grade will be based on this examination; the remaining seventy-five percent will be based on the number of units of reading and laboratory work that you have successfully completed during the term."

Along with this description and a few items of further information or instruction, the student is given his first reading assignment. This assignment not only designates the actual pages of textbook or other reading to be done, but also points up topics of special importance, it clarifies those that may be inadequately covered, and it provides material for linking one work unit with another. In addition, there is a set of study questions, running to thirty or forty in number. These are intended to sample every element of the reading for which the student will be held responsible. If he can find the correct answers to these questions and retain them, he will come to the testing situation with a high probability of passing his first quiz on any study unit.

When the student receives his reading assignment and his study questions, he is ready to begin work. The main classroom is available as a study-hall during scheduled hours, usually with a member of the staff present for consultation. A smaller room, also with a staff member in charge, serves for test-taking. A third room, in which there are ten proctors' cubicles, is set aside for the grading and discussion of tests. When a student feels himself prepared for examination at any time during the class hour, he picks up a number at the study-hall desk and awaits his turn for testing. When a place is free, he goes to the testing room, where he receives his test and his blue book from the person in charge. When he has answered the questions, he returns the test, but keeps his blue book and goes immediately to one of the cubicles in the proctor's room. When the test has been graded by his proctor, the student is given his next assignment or is sent back to study for a later test on the same unit, usually after considerable discussion of the errors made. The graded test is kept by the proctor, who passes it on at the end of the period to the assistant or the instructor, for checking and recording.

The readiness tests themselves are commonly composed of ten or more questions, mainly of the sentence-completion type, together with one short essay question. For each unit, there are alternate test forms, ranging in number from three to six. After the first five units, each new unit test is accompanied by a *review test* on an earlier unit. These review tests are similar to the original ones, but shorter, and they too must be passed successfully before the student can go ahead.

Once a week throughout the term, the proctors meet with the assistant and the instructor, to go over the preceding week's work and prepare for the next. This meeting deals mainly with problems arising from unclear study material, with test questions that have caused special trouble, and with acceptable answers to the questions that will be used in later tests. Textbook flaws that may have gone for years without discovery are often exposed by this procedure; and bad test questions turn up regularly in spite of long experience of test construction. The number of different interpretations that can be given to a perfectly clear and unambiguous question is appalling. When a perfect score is desired of every student before permitting him to go ahead, one learns to look upon quizzing in a brand new way.

The selection of proctors is made from undergraduates who have taken the same course, or one with similar content, in an earlier term, and who have been promised two points of academic credit for satisfactory discharge of their proctorial duties. Initially, we sought junior or senior majors in psychology, with graduate-school intentions, but we were unable to get enough of these to meet our proctor-student ratio of one to ten. We have been forced to take non-majors, sophomores, and, in a few instances, second-term freshmen. Under adequate supervision, a well-motivated A-student, even in his first year of college, is likely to meet the requirements of the job without appreciable difficulty. If his preparation leaves something to be desired at the time of assuming his duties, this will quickly be repaired through contact with the earliest students to pass through his hands — students who are generally the best ones in the class. Even a mediocre proctor, at the beginning of his work, may be an expert by the time his skill is really needed.

Lectures, demonstrations, and the like are announced well in advance and by title. Admission fee is specified in terms of course units passed, and every attempt is made to have them as rewarding as possible. By ordinary standards, they are short and infrequent. A well-planned twenty-minute performance at the beginning of a scheduled study-hall hour, perhaps once in every two or three weeks, will cause a surge in test-taking and will draw a modest crowd when given, if testing is suspended while the show is on.

Students in the course are at all times aware of their progress, either from their own records of tests passed and experiments completed or from charts provided by the classroom assistant. Each student should know where he is and where he ought to be, with respect to work-units completed, but the burden of responsibility for study and test-taking is placed squarely upon his own shoulders. No goading, no exhorting, no chiding, no promising or threatening of any sort is resorted to at any time. If the student wants to pass the course, he knows what to do. He will receive personal attention and consideration at every step along the way, but he must make the step himself.

The learning situation that I have just described is similar in several ways to that provided in the field of teaching machines, programmed textbooks, and computer-based instruction. There is the same stress upon initial analysis and organization of the subject matter to be taught; there is the same concern with the terminal behavior to be established in the repertory of each student; the same provision for individualized advancement when clearly specified requirements have been satisfied; and the same possibility of program self-correction on the basis of student reactions.

The sphere of action in this course, however, is much larger. It approximates the total educational process. The steps of advance are not "frames" in a "set." They resemble more closely the usual homework or laboratory assignment. The "response" upon which a student's progress depends is not simply the completion of a prepared statement through the insertion of a word or phrase. Rather, it may be thought of as the resultant of many such responses, better described as the understanding of a principle, a formula, a concept, or the ability to use an experimental technique. Advance within the program depends on something more than the appearance of a confirming word or the presentation of a new frame; it involves a personal interaction between a student and his peer, or his better, in what may be lively verbal interchange, of interest and importance to each participant. The use of a programmed text, a teaching machine, or some sort of computer aid *within* such a course is entirely possible and may be quite desirable, but is not to be equated with the course itself.

If I were now to list those features of our method which distinguish it from conventional procedures within a mass education framework, I would have to include:

1. *The go-at-your-own-pace feature* which permits a student to move through the course at a speed commensurate with his ability and other demands upon his time.

2. *The unit-perfection requirement for advance*, which lets the student go ahead to new material only after demonstrating mastery of that which preceded.

3. *The use of lectures and demonstrations as vehicles of motivation*, rather than sources of critical information.

4. *The related stress upon the written word* in teacher-student communication.

5. *The use of proctors*, which permits repeated testing, immediate scoring, almost unavoidable tutoring, and a marked enhancement of the personal-social aspect of the educational process.

The reaction of our students to this method of instruction during the past few terms has been almost unanimously favorable. During the second term, shortly before the end of classes, a twenty-item questionnaire was given to all those students, ninety-four in number, who were present at one of the regular class periods. This questionnaire, in which the students did not need to reveal their identity, showed considerable agreement on a number of points. In comparison with conventional procedures, this method requires a *greater amount of work*, produces a *greater degree of understanding of the course content*, generates a *greater feeling of achievement*, and provides a *greater recognition of the student as a person*. The feeling was also expressed by many students that their study habits had improved as the term went on, even in unrelated courses, and that their *attitude toward test-taking had become much more positive*. With respect to the student-proctor relation, nearly everyone reported that the *discussion of tests with the proctors was helpful*, or *very helpful*. About ten percent of the group volunteered the comment that other courses should be conducted in similar fashion.

Such reactions confirmed the opinions already formed by the

staff at one time or another during the semester. It was obvious to all of us that our method, even in its crude, unpolished form, produced an unusually high degree of educational control. At first, this control appeared to have aversive overtones. The testing was frequent, inevitable, and rigorous; the procedure was unusual, lacking in all customary constraints; and there was a prevailing air of uncertainty about events to come. Within a few weeks, however, the general atmosphere was one of industry, orderliness, and good humor. There was an obvious pride of accomplishment, among the slow students as well as the fast. Testing itself appeared to be welcomed, even enjoyed, and getting a new assignment was like receiving a badge of honor. Interest in passing tests got to be so great that it interfered with lecture attendance, and we were led to reduce the lecture time and stop all test-taking while a lecture was in progress. It led us also to introduce a two-hour testing period on every Saturday morning — a fixture of the course that has become permanent.

As for proctors and assistants, their attitude has also been positive. The proctors, in particular, claim to derive benefit from several sources: the review of study materials and questions in preparation for test grading and discussion; the discussions themselves, in which their understanding is tested and their skill in expression is improved; and in the weekly staff sessions, wherein a great deal of incidental instruction takes place as we examine the problems that have been met with in the past or that are likely to come up in the future. One of my colleagues recently referred to our proctors as an "elite corps" of students at this educational level. I believe that this is true, and that they have also come to have a rich awareness of the problems and pleasures of teaching.

The duties of an instructor, in a course like this, are quite demanding of time and effort, especially during the period in which the course is being formed. Initially, he must decide upon its content. Then he must break down this content into *tentative* units of instruction — tentative because he cannot be sure, at the beginning, that these units are comparable in difficulty or realistic in scope. Never before has he required that all his students learn an assignment to the point of complete mastery. At first, he must therefore "play by ear," leaning heavily upon his experience with similar materials in a more conventional context of instruction.

He must know the content of his course in more intimate detail than he ever has before. Three hundred study questions, or more, and perhaps two thousand test questions, will be based upon this material. In addition, he may have to write supplements for unclear or incomplete portions of it, or portions in which he may find errors. These supplements, to be effective, must be written with unusual clarity. They will be subjected to unusual scrutiny, and they will no longer be accompanied by explanatory lectures. The instructor's writing is therefore likely to improve, and he may find himself composing a textbook of his own — little by little, with corrective feed-back at every step. This is done, however, as a part of his everyday teaching function, rather than in those hard-won periods that could otherwise be devoted to research or recreation.

I do not need to tell this audience that there is nothing new about any of the elements of the method I have been describing. The use of students in the teaching of other students within a schoolroom setting goes back to the late 18th and early 19th centuries, where it appeared in the "mutual tuition" and "monitorial" systems of elementary education made famous by Andrew Bell (1753-1832) and Joseph Lancaster (1778-1883). It was also present in the "pupil-teacher" system that replaced them. The go-at-your-own-pace procedure has been used, even with large numbers, in certain areas of practical education, as in military training centers. Here, too, the teaching staff may be composed of former pupils, and perfection of the skill is vital to success, and sometimes to survival. Teaching without lectures is an obvious feature of correspondence-school instruction, and so is a highly individualized student-teacher relationship.

Even in its totality, the method has been anticipated. This I discovered with some surprise in a recent book by C. W. Washburn and S. P. Marland, Jr., entitled *Winnetka: The History and Significance of an Educational Experiment*.[3] In this book, the story is told of an experiment conducted more than fifty years ago at the San Francisco State Normal School, under the presidency of Dr. Frederic Burk, a highly regarded educator of that period. The parallel with our own method is so striking that I am going to take a moment to describe the study here.

Students at this normal school began their practice teaching soon after they arrived, working under the surveillance of supervisors in the different areas of elementary instruction. Two practice teachers were assigned to each class of twenty children. Each supervisor had four such classes, with two practice teachers in each.

One of the supervisors was Mary Ward, a teacher of arithmetic. During a discussion with her practice teachers, one day after class, it was pointed out that the study materials then in use were too hard for some children and too easy for others. Miss Ward suggested that they prepare materials suited to each of three groups—the slow, the average, and the fast. This was done, and the situation improved, but it was soon discovered that, within each group, there were still important differences. The slower children had different degrees of retardation, the faster ones different degrees of acceleration, and the "average" spread from almost retarded to almost accelerated.

Before long, Miss Ward and her practice teachers were preparing materials for each individual child. It appeared that, if these materials were suitable for one child, every other child could use them, although at different times. The result, by the end of the year, was a wide range of achievement within the group. The fastest child had done two years' work—twice as much as the slowest child.

Miss Ward reported her findings to Dr. Burk, who immediately "caught fire." He had her describe her experiment to the faculty and he proposed that every supervisor should prepare comparable study materials for his own subject and classes. If written simply and clearly enough, each child could almost "teach himself" with such materials, although the student teacher could always be on hand to help when needed. The proposal was accepted and the supervisors, with their student teachers, began the preparation of "self-instruction bulletins."

These "bulletins" were used at first in conjunction with the teachers' textbooks. They specified the material to be studied, they amplified and clarified where necessary, and they sometimes included supplementary materials. They were given to the classes in mimeographed form and, after one year's tryout, were subjected to revision on the basis of student reaction. In time, they became the only course materials and were even adopted for use in other schools.

From then on, instruction in elementary classes at this normal school was conducted on an individual basis. Each child moved at his own pace, neither hurried nor delayed by the other children. Also, the idea spread in various directions, in this country and abroad. Perhaps it spread too rapidly and with too little understanding of the essential features, or combination of features, that made it effective.

In 1912, when all this happened, the scientific study of learning had scarcely begun. Neither Mary Ward nor any other teacher of her day could have profited very much from a detailed acquaintance with everything then known in this important area. Neither she nor anyone else could have recognized the operation, in her classroom, of behavior principles that are now well established.

Today, the scene has changed. Within the past four decades, the science of psychology has made some giant steps forward in the prediction, the control, and the interpretation of human conduct.

This has been due to the development of new research tactics and a new systematic formulation. The research tactics have opened up the whole field of "voluntary" behavior to scientific treatment. The systematic formulation, which often goes by the name of *reinforcement theory*, is an integration of facts and principles derived from this new treatment.

Reinforcement theory provided the systematic background for those of us who initiated this self-paced, personalized, or proctorial method of teaching which is the burden of my talk today. Every aspect of our method was discussed and evaluated, from start to finish, in terms of reinforcement and reinforcement contingencies. I won't go into all this here, but I would like to count off, in non-technical language, some of (perhaps *most* of) the rewards for educational behavior that operate within our method. We believe that these rewards are directly responsible for the degree of educational control we have achieved.

First, for the student, there are the rewards attendant upon moving ahead, unit by unit, up to the course's end. Some of these are not particularly strong; they vary with the individual student in their importance; and they are not peculiar to our method. For example, there are the rewards that come from moving into new and sometimes interesting territory; from the discovery of new relations between facts and principles, old or new; and from finding practical applications of laboratory science. But getting ahead is supported in other ways, less conventionally, or at least in greater degree than is common in present-day teaching. It guarantees the privilege of attending a lecture, a demonstration, or a movie. It may give almost complete assurance of a final *A*, which may in turn guarantee the continuance of a scholarship, admittance to some social group, eligibility to stay in college or engage in sports, or freedom to do other things at the end of the term. Getting ahead is also supported, at almost every step, by signs of respect from one's classmates, the approval of one's proctor, or a word of congratulation from an assistant or the instructor—all of which are common in the system.

The most important of the new rewards are those provided by the proctors. The proctor is a member of the peer group. He is just another student, but he has a special status, and he is more closely associated with labor than with management. He is an advanced student, but not so advanced as to be remote, or to be lacking in memory of the problems that he and his friends have met in passing the course. He (or she) is commonly a pleasant, attractive person, well regarded within the university, whose acquaintance and good opinion might also be sought in a non-academic setting. He is almost always helpful and almost never complaining. He is obviously pleased when one of his charges does well on a test, but he is also ready to commiserate, to counsel, or advise in the event of a failure. For an occasional student, he may be the only regular social contact within the university community. It is not hard to see why a student may write that, "in this course I wasn't just a face in a crowd." Or, "I didn't just feel like a number on a page but like an individual student."

From such rewards as these, motivation emerges almost automatically. Even if it did not, there would be another source. There is another side to the coin of getting ahead — an almost unavoidable kind of aversive control. When a student passes his unit test, the new assignment he receives is not only a recognition of work well done, it is also a challenge to perform successfully again. It is in some degree a *threat* that will only be reduced when the next test is passed. The study questions of each assignment also possess this quality; each one is a little hurdle that must be cleared before one goes ahead. (Even an item in a readiness test may set up a tiny tension that won't be reduced until a satisfactory answer comes.) And behind these lesser threats, backing them up, lie the greater ones — the threat of lost approval, lost prestige, lost privilege, and lost assurance of a final *A*.

This sort of influence is especially apparent in the early phases of a student's work, before this test-taking has become so much a matter of sideplaying his control of the subject matter. But it reappears later, quite vividly, say after a period of absence or when a student fails two, or sometimes three, tests in succession. Anxiety then becomes pronounced, even to the point of disrupting normal test-taking behavior. In fact, it is difficult to say with any assurance that the student's attainment of a positive state of affairs is more rewarding than his elimination of a negative one. Both kinds are often apparent in student reports concerning the amount of pressure placed upon them by the method. The number of students who report *very little* is matched closely by the number who report *very much*. While one student writes that the method "put undue pressure upon me to go faster than I would have liked," another says that it "relieved me from worry and tension. I knew where I stood. I could take the tests when I had time to prepare adequately."

The aversive aspects of our control are unfortunate, perhaps, but they are inevitable, and they do not outweigh the positive features. Nor do they compare in importance with those that exist on many occasions and for many students under conventional modes of instruction. Think of the worries that may be generated in a conscientious student when he misses a lecture, a demonstration, a laboratory meeting, or a test, for any reason whatever, good or bad. Or when he attends a lecture and loses some important part of it because he was distracted by some interruption, or even because he let himself become engrossed in an idea raised by the speaker's words. Or consider the situation when a student is unable to understand a reading assignment, and the teacher doesn't clarify the issue. Or when he gets a low grade on a test, and knows that it will affect his final grade; when he gets little or no opportunity to defend his answer to a question; or when he is unable, generally, to get any form of personal attention to his problems. No one of these items is alone a source of great trouble perhaps, but when you sum them up and multiply them by the number of courses a student is taking, when you add extraneous pressures that call upon him to succeed at least in some degree within the system, and when you cap the total (as sometimes happens) by blaming the student for the mess he is in, you encourage frustration, resentment, anger, escape behavior, or even destruction.

What are the proctors' rewards in such a method as ours? It is obvious that the proctors like their work. They are seldom absent from their posts; they sometimes volunteer for extra duty; they will expatiate to strangers on the method's merits; and their complaints are almost always limited to minor aspects of their function. But if you ask them to identify the rewards that keep them at their jobs, you may get no very satisfying answers. "I liked the method when I took the course, and now I like proctoring." "It gives you a lot of control." "Maybe it's because you like to help others." "I'm a psychology major." "You really learn what you have to explain," and so on.

Some of the proctor's rewards are so obvious as to go unnoticed, or be thought unworthy of mention. For example, everything the proctor says or does in carrying out his duties is the occasion for the student's undivided *attention*. This may be less important for some proctors than for others, and it may depend upon the source but it probably has some meaning for everyone. In addition, it is often coupled with a respectful attitude on the part of the student — an understanding nod, a responsive smile, or a word of agreement. There is *submission* to the proctor's judgment and courting the proctor's *approval*. The proctor may also be an object of gratitude and affection, by virtue of his position in the chain of getting ahead activities, or for other reasons. Social psychologists have stressed the importance of such factors under the heading of human *needs*— the need for attention, for approval, for power, for affection, and so on — they are all present in this situation.

There are still other rewards for the proctor, which are not provided by the student. There is the consideration he receives from his instructor; the improvement in his status as a student; the commendation he may receive from his family; and the two points of *A* that may be added to his grade average.

The proctor's life, however, is not entirely without aversive features. The record of his judgments, his passings and failings, is always being examined by the assistant or the instructor. Over-generosity in grading, or over-severity, is quickly brought to his attention. His explanations or recommendations to a student may be overheard and noted, and subjected to later correction. If one of his charges fails too often, it will cause him to worry, for his success as a proctor depends in some degree upon the success of his students, and so on; but the continued enthusiasm of the proctor for his work suggests that the positive features of his task far outweigh the negative. We now have more candidates for the job than we have openings.

It was once written of Andrew Bell, the inventor and avid promoter of the system of "mutual tuition," in which children were employed in the teaching of other children, that "his own eagerness made other people all the more ready to disallow his claims." Some comment of this sort applies to me. I didn't invent it, but I am obviously too enthusiastic about the merits of this "proctorial" system. What about its defects, its limitations, its objective validation, and the like? Such questions are certain to be asked by critics and they deserve an answer.

Our method has had imperfections since its earliest tryouts. Some have been corrected, entirely or in part; others have not. I'll mention two or three, but there may be more. One source of concern, from time to time, has been that of *cheating*. At present, our procedures make this highly improbable, but the possibility of a dishonest proctor cannot be ruled out entirely. Related to this is the fact that some proctors are "easier" than others, sometimes permitting insufficiently qualified students to move ahead. These are faults, in spite of the fact that they are almost certain to be discovered and corrected.

A more serious defect of the method at this time lies in the percentage of *failures* or *drop-outs* that it may produce. Ideally, given the grade of *Incomplete*, one hundred percent of the students in the course should pass with an *A*. Practically, this has never been achieved. In the best of my classes, only forty percent received the *A* as a final grade. Twenty percent took the *Incomplete*, but only half of them completed the course in the following year. Nineteen percent either failed or withdrew from the course. Most of the remainder received *B*'s. Although the percentage of failures and withdrawals is not much different from that which existed under the old system, it does raise the question of remedial treatment for at least some of the students. In a conventional lecture and laboratory course, you always cherish the notion that a failure or drop-out learned *something*, although you can't say what. In this type of course, you may know exactly what he learned, but it may be nothing.

Another possible weakness and source of worry is the fact that the top students in a course like this do not have an opportunity to engage regularly with the instructor in classroom give-and-take, or pick up the informational extras that three lectures a week might provide. For those students who later become proctors, there will be no great loss, but one cannot be sure that the absence of such an opportunity for other students will be offset entirely by their improved mastery of the course assignments. If this defect is real, there may be no good remedy for it at this rung of the educational ladder.

Where is the evidence that our method is better than any other in the kind of educational results it produces? This is a deceptively simple question, and there is no single answer. Not even a compound answer would satisfy everyone. It is not enough to say that in forty years of teaching I have never enjoyed myself so much before; it won't add much to point to a grade distribution that contains more *A*'s than anything else; and nothing very important will be gained by referring to the overwhelmingly positive reactions of students to the items of a questionnaire.

It might be more convincing to show that a group of students trained by our method would perform better on some tests than a group of students trained more conventionally. The two groups would be exposed to the same course content, equated with respect to sources of error, and tested with a suitable examination.

One such comparison has already been made; another is going on this week, at Queens College,[4] in New York; and at least two others are being planned elsewhere. The results of the first one, comparing students at Arizona State University with students at one of the Ivy League colleges in the East, support the new procedure very strongly, in spite of bias that would favor the Eastern school.

Too much emphasis should not be placed on such comparisons. If a procedure is still undergoing change, as is ours, they are premature; we might rather be doing something else. If it is fully developed, we are probably executing a *tour de force*, its superiority has been obvious to us all along. If we expect someone to adopt a method by showing him a statistically significant difference, we are doomed to failure; his decision will be based on many factors, including several that I haven't mentioned. I can imagine adopting a procedure that I knew to be less effective than another in the teaching of subject matter.

The possibilities of extending our method to other disciplines and at other educational levels are largely unknown. Success has been reported with high school juniors, at one extreme, and the professional staff of a large state hospital and training school, at the other.[5] A modification of the procedure has been used effectively in teaching elementary statistics;[6] and plans are currently being made for a computer-assisted course in educational psychology, a course in physics for Junior College teachers, and an engineering school course in analytical mechanics. There may be other applications, but I don't know of them.

Thirty years ago, while attending a conference at Dartmouth

College, I went with a friend to the college library to see Orozco's famous frescos. The picture that most impressed me was that of a delivery room, in which a birth was taking place. The participants in the event, as well as a few observers in the background, were alike in two respects: they were skeletons and they were dressed in cap and gown. The title of the fresco, as I later learned, was *Alma Mater*.

Today, I can read into this painting a statement of the lack of fundamental change in educational practices within the lifetime of the artist; and I can add another generation to his own, in which nothing of great importance has been contributed to our methods of teaching.

This cannot go on forever. Our knowledge of the learning process has advanced too far for that. One breakthrough has appeared already with the advent of programmed instruction, in 1958; but this was only a beginning. More revolutionary things will happen, must happen, if we are to educate effectively within a democratic society.

The method I've described today is certainly not the final answer to our problem. I think it does reflect, however, a widely-shared and growing concern of behavioral scientists with the ancient art of teaching; and it may be a harbinger of things to come.